Unlocking the Mysteries of Birth and Death

...and everything in between

SECOND EDITION

Daisaku Ikeda

MIDDLEWAY
PRESS

Published by Middleway Press
A division of the SGI-USA
606 Wilshire Blvd.
Santa Monica, CA 90401

First English edition published in Great Britain in 1988 by
Macdonald & Co. (Publishers) Ltd.
London & Sydney

ISBN 0-9723267-0-7

Design by Gopa & Ted2, Inc.

10   9   8   7   6   5   4   3   2

Library of Congress Cataloging-in-Publication Data

Ikeda, Daisaku.
    Unlocking the mysteries of birth and death / Daisaku Ikeda.
    p. cm.
    ISBN 0-9723267-0-7 (Paperback : alk. paper)

    1. Soka Gakkai--Doctrines. I. Title.
BQ8449.I384U65 2003
294.3'420428--dc22

                                        2003021963

Contents

Preface

A S THE AUTHOR, I am extremely happy that Middleway Press is publishing this revised edition of *Unlocking the Mysteries of Birth and Death*. Death, which is a major theme of the book, is the inevitable reality of life, and the two phases of life and death constitute an inescapable law for all beings. Confronting death at a fundamental level is an inevitable spiritual undertaking that helps us to live more profoundly and more meaningfully.

As the Latin phrase *memento mori*—remember that you must die—suggests, we grasp the true meaning of life only when we honestly face the reality of death. Two and a half millennia ago, the desire to overcome the basic human sufferings of birth, aging, illness and death motivated the historical Buddha, Shakyamuni, to abandon his princely rank and undertake the search for truth. Buddhism originated with his enlightenment, which revealed the ultimate law of life as the foundation of the universe and the inner human cosmos. The Buddhist teachings developed and were expounded in many scriptures, from early Buddhism through Mahayana Buddhism, but the essence of them all is the Lotus Sutra, which explains the potential Buddhahood—the Buddha nature—inherent in everyone.

Over the course of the ages, Buddhism traveled southward

from India to Sri Lanka, Burma, Thailand and Cambodia. In its northward movement, it passed through Central Asia, China and the Korean Peninsula to reach Japan, where Nichiren was born in the thirteenth century. Nichiren taught the ultimate expression of Shakyamuni's enlightenment in the form of the universal Law, Nam-myoho-renge-kyo. In addition, he developed the distinctive Nichiren Buddhism, which subsumes the teachings and philosophies of such teachers as the Indians Nagarjuna (second or third century) and Vasubandhu (fourth or fifth century) and the Chinese T'ien-t'ai (Tiantai; 538–597). Nichiren Buddhism puts the teachings of the Lotus Sutra into actual practice for the sake of ordinary people. Indeed, Nichiren referred to himself as a practitioner of the Lotus Sutra.

Astonishing developments in science and technology make the world we live in today entirely different from the one Nichiren knew. To bridge the gap, this book attempts to set up a dialogue between our times and the foundation of Nichiren Buddhism. Its contents represent a partial explanation of the contributions that Nichiren's teachings can make to the future of humanity by providing a clear perspective on today's world and helping us know how to interpret contemporary philosophy, science and the universe itself.

Though seven centuries old, the Buddhism of Nichiren provides a marvelous prescription for the helplessness and despair now pervading society. Fate, of course, does not always turn out according to our wishes, but Buddhism—especially Nichiren Buddhism—possesses the power with which we can transform destiny. It sheds light on all aspects of human life and penetrates to its core. Universally applicable to all humanity, in every circumstance, it is well worth lifelong study and application.

Conditions for individuals, society and the world at large

have changed dramatically during the fifteen years that have
passed since the first English-language edition of this book. As
many thinkers point out, in the past, little development took
place in the way humanity regarded life and death. Astonishing
advances in science, however, have stimulated the desire for
new views on life and death.

Newly discovered scientific facts, as well as new perspectives
on life and death, are taken into consideration in this revised
edition, which includes various additions, corrections and
improvements in the translation. Nichiren's teachings emphasize the dignity of human life—the Buddha nature or fundamental universal life—inherent in humanity. I have taken great
care to transmit an accurate understanding of this philosophy in
contemporary terms.

Since my youth I have loved the nineteenth-century American poet Walt Whitman, whose work contains praise for life
itself and interpretations of the cosmos and nature that correspond with Buddhist views. For instance, his "Song of the Universal" includes the following passage:

> Come said the Muse,
> Sing me a song no poet yet has chanted,
> Sing me the universal.
>
> In the broad earth of ours,
> Amid the measureless grossness and the slag,
> Enclosed and safe within its central heart,
> Nestles the seed perfection.

I am certain that readers of this book will discover in Buddhist philosophy a new approach to what Whitman calls "the
universal." Nothing could make me happier than for this book

to provide an opportunity to learn, to discover and to undertake major self-revolution.

Finally, let me express my deepest gratitude to Middleway Press, the staff of the Soka Gakkai Study Department, and the many other people whose tireless efforts made this revised edition possible.

Daisaku Ikeda
November 18, 2003

Introduction

WE ALL DESIRE HAPPINESS, and yet happiness
always seems to be just beyond our reach.
Numerous philosophers have tackled the question of happiness. Without exception, I believe their conclusions have been incomplete. However many "how to be happy" books might appear, human beings are still largely beset by the same problems as their ancestors. The poor seek wealth, the sick yearn to be healthy, those suffering from domestic strife crave harmony, and so on. Even if we secure wealth, health and a happy home life, we inevitably find ourselves confronted by problems in other areas. Furthermore, should we somehow fashion circumstances that apparently satisfy all the conditions necessary for happiness, how long can we maintain those circumstances? Obviously not forever. Few of us can avoid the illnesses and slow weakening of the body that accompany aging, and none of us can escape death.

Problems, however, are not in themselves the fundamental cause of unhappiness. According to Buddhism, the real cause is not just that we have problems but that we lack the power and wisdom to solve them. Buddhism teaches that all individuals innately possess infinite power and wisdom, and it reveals the process whereby these qualities can be developed. In addressing the issue of happiness, Buddhism focuses not so much on eliminating suffering and difficulties, which are understood to be inherent in life, as on how we should cultivate the potentials that exist within us. Strength and wisdom, Buddhism explains, derive from life force. If we cultivate sufficient life force, we can not only withstand life's adversities but transform them into causes of happiness and empowerment.

If this is to be our goal, however, we must first identify the principal sufferings of life. Buddhism describes four universal sufferings — birth, aging, sickness and death. No matter how much we would like to cling to our youth, we age with the passage of time. Try as we might to maintain good health, we will eventually contract some disease or other ailment. And, more fundamentally, though we abhor the thought of dying, any moment could be our last (although, of course, it is beyond our power to know when that moment will come).

We can recognize various causes — biological, physiological and psychological — for the sufferings of sickness, aging and death. But ultimately it is life itself, our birth into this world, that is the cause of all our mundane sufferings.

In Sanskrit, suffering is called *duhkha*, a word implying a state fraught with difficulty in which people and things do not accord with our wishes. This condition derives from the fact that all phenomena are transient. Youth and health do not continue forever, nor can our very lives themselves. Here, according to Buddhism, lies the ultimate cause of human suffering.

Shakyamuni, or the historical Gautama Buddha, renounced the secular world after encountering these worldy sufferings in what's known as the four meetings, a story found in many Buddhist scriptures. So that the young Shakyamuni, known as Prince Siddhartha, would be shielded from worldly suffering, his father, King Shuddhodana, essentially confined him to the palace. Emerging from the east gate of the palace one day, however, he encountered a withered old man tottering along with a cane. Seeing this man, Shakyamuni deeply recognized how life inevitably entails the suffering of aging. On another occasion, leaving the palace by the south gate, he saw a sick person and realized that sickness, too, is a part of life. A third time, leaving via the west gate, he saw a corpse; this "meeting" led him to grasp the reality that all which lives must eventually die. Finally, exiting the north gate one day, he encountered a religious ascetic whose air of serene dignity awoke in the prince a resolve to embark on a religious life.

Eventually, after dedicating himself for many years to various religious practices, ascetic and otherwise, Shakyamuni attained enlightenment, gaining freedom from the sufferings of birth, aging, sickness and death. Determined to lead other people to this enlightenment, he set about preaching and came to be known as the "Buddha," a Sanskrit term meaning an "enlightened one" — a person whose wisdom encompasses the ultimate truth of life and the universe.

It is generally held that, immediately after his enlightenment, Shakyamuni preached the doctrines of the four noble truths and the eightfold path. The four noble truths are:

✦ the truth of suffering

✦ the truth of the origin of suffering

✦ the truth of the cessation of suffering

✦ the truth of the path to the cessation of suffering

The *truth of suffering* is that all existence in this world entails suffering, as represented by the four sufferings we have noted as being inherent in life. The *truth of the origin of suffering* states that suffering is caused by selfish craving for the ephemeral pleasures of the world. The *truth of the cessation of suffering* is that the eradication of this selfish craving ends the suffering. And *the truth of the path to the cessation of suffering* is that there exists a path by which this eradication can be achieved. That path is traditionally interpreted as the discipline of the eightfold path. This latter is composed of:

+ right views, based on the four noble truths and a correct understanding of Buddhism

+ right thinking, or command of one's mind

+ right speech

+ right action

+ right way of life, based on purifying one's thoughts, words and deeds

+ right endeavor, to seek the true Law

+ right mindfulness, always to bear right views in mind

+ right meditation

The four noble truths and the eightfold path were directed chiefly to those disciples who had rejected secular life and were wholly engaged in Buddhist practice; they reflect the basic attitude and approach that underlie Shakyamuni's early teachings, which concentrated on predominantly negative views about life and the world so that he could awaken people first to life's harsh realities and then to the inexpressible spiritual experience of nirvana. If carried out to the letter, these teachings, which encouraged the negation of all desires, would inevitably lead to the negation of the desire to live. The fundamental solution to

human suffering in this world, accordingly, lies in the eradication of earthly desires — that is, all manner of desire, impulse
and passion arising from the depths of people's lives. By following these teachings, people could allegedly sever their ties to
the cycle of birth and death and attain the state wherein rebirth
in this world is no longer necessary — that is, they could attain
the state of nirvana.

While these teachings may have been applicable and beneficial to monks and nuns, they were extremely difficult for lay
people to follow. Shakyamuni's original determination, however, was to lead every human being on this earth to happiness.
For this reason, he traveled back and forth across the Middle
Ganges region, expounding his philosophy. But lay people, even
if they wanted to achieve nirvana, must have found it not just
impracticable but actually impossible to abandon all earthly
desires. They had families to support, jobs to do, and other
everyday affairs that demanded their attention. While nirvana
might have been an ideal, it was in no way an attainable goal.
Somehow, though, Shakyamuni's wisdom and compassion
always reached the ordinary people who, obviously, had many
problems that they lacked the means to solve. Had this not been
the case — had Buddhism been unable to help ordinary people
— then it would never have achieved a status higher than that
of an intellectual pursuit. Shakyamuni counseled people and
inspired them with hope and courage so that they could overcome their sufferings and enjoy the prospect of a brilliant future.
For example, he spoke about a pure land far from this world
where, by following his teachings, people could be reborn free
from all desires and strangers to any suffering or fear.

Just as he encouraged his monks and nuns to observe his
many precepts and follow the eightfold path in order to attain
nirvana, Shakyamuni taught his lay believers to be faithful to

his teachings so that they could be reborn into the pure land. But, in actuality, neither the eradication of desire nor rebirth in the pure land is attainable. It is impossible to blow out the fires of desire and interrupt the cycle of birth and death because desire is inherent in life, life is eternal, and birth and death are the inescapable alternating aspects of life. Nor is it possible to reach a pure land that does not in fact exist. Both nirvana and the pure land were metaphorical devices employed by Shakyamuni to develop his followers' understanding.

From another perspective, the teaching concerning nirvana was directed toward personal emancipation through the realization of ultimate truth, and the pure land teaching was directed toward the emancipation of the people at large. These teachings are representative of the two major streams of Buddhism — the ascetic traditions from early Buddhism and the altruistic, popular movements called Mahayana (the great vehicle) — and were later integrated in the Lotus Sutra, which we shall discuss at some length in this book. The Lotus Sutra makes it absolutely clear that two aspects of Buddhist practice are indispensable if we are to attain enlightenment. One is directed toward perfecting ourselves, in the sense that we realize the ultimate truth and develop our inherent potential, and the other is the practice of leading people toward that perfection.

The Lotus Sutra also reveals the true meanings of nirvana and the pure land. According to the sutra, we do not have to stop the cycle of birth and death in order to enter nirvana. Rather, nirvana is the state of enlightenment in which, as we repeat the cycle of birth and death, we come to terms with that cycle and it no longer is a source of suffering. Similarly, we do not have to abandon all desire in order to attain nirvana because we can transform earthly desires into causes of happiness and, further, of enlightened wisdom. Moreover, the pure land does not necessarily lie beyond death. We dwell in the pure land here and now if we believe in the Lotus Sutra, which reveals that we can transform this world — filled as it is with suffering and sorrow — into a pure land full of joy and hope.

Some Fundamental Doctrines

How exactly does Buddhism provide the solution to the fundamental problems of life and death? By taking a close look at each of the four sufferings — birth, aging, sickness and death — this book seeks to illuminate the truth and wisdom necessary to sail calmly over the troubled sea of worldly suffering.

At no time in the past has science been in a state of such rapid advancement. As a result, humanity has adopted a blind belief in the powers of science and technology, regarding the problems inherent in life less from the viewpoints of philosophy and religion. Observing the global state of affairs today, I cannot help feeling that people are not grappling hard enough with fundamental problems.

From the perspective of ultimate truth, earthly desires and the problems of life and death are not seen as obstacles that must be eradicated. Instead, earthly desires can be transformed into enlightened wisdom, and the sufferings of birth and death are means to attaining nirvana. The Lotus Sutra takes this one step further, setting forth the principles that earthly desires *are* enlightenment and that the sufferings of birth and death *are* nirvana. In other words, there can be no enlightenment apart from the reality of earthly desires and there can be no nirvana without the concomitant sufferings of birth and death. These pairs of contrasting factors are innate in all our lives.

T'ien-t'ai, the great sixth-century Chinese teacher, employed an analogy to explain the above principles. Suppose there is a bitter persimmon. By soaking it in a solution of lime or buck-wheat chaff, or by exposing it to sunlight, we can make the persimmon sweet. There are not two persimmons, one bitter and the other sweet — there is only the one. The bitter persimmon has not been sweetened with sugar; rather, the inherent bitterness of the persimmon has been drawn out and its inherent sweetness allowed to emerge. The catalyst, the intermediary that assisted the transformation, was the solution or the sunlight. T'ien-t'ai likened earthly desires to the bitter persimmon, enlightenment to the sweet persimmon, and the process whereby the sweetness was brought out to Buddhist practice.

To fully benefit from these important doctrines in our daily lives, we must comprehend some basic Buddhist teachings, which illumine life's multifaceted dimensions. Toward that end, we shall examine two major doctrines — "three thousand realms in a single moment of life" and "the nine consciousnesses" — which represent the pinnacle of Mahayana Buddhism. Instead of negating desire and life in this world, they accept the realities of life as they are and reveal the way to transform them into causes of enlightenment. The profound doctrine that earthly desires are enlightenment teaches that we should not try to eradicate desires or regard them as sinful, but should elevate them toward achieving a nobler state of life.

The Ten Worlds

For a correct understanding of the Buddhist view of life, the concept of the Ten Worlds is indispensable. The first six of the Ten Worlds derive from the idea of the six paths, an ancient Indian paradigm concerning transmigration: these six worlds, or paths, are the worlds of hell, hungry spirits (Hunger), animals (Animality), *asuras* (Anger), humans (Humanity) and heavenly beings (Heaven). It was thought that the particular world or realm into which unenlightened people were born was determined by the things they had done in past lifetimes, and that people endlessly repeated the cycle of birth and death in these six worlds. Even if born into the highest world, Heaven, one could not stay there long; when good fortune was exhausted, the individual would fall back into a lower state of existence.

Transmigration in the six paths could be likened to moving from floor to floor inside a six-story building shut off from the outside. The floor corresponding to Heaven is at the top and beneath it are the floors representing the other worlds, all the way down to Hell on the ground floor. Each floor is connected to each of the others. People are confined in this building, going up and down forever. Even though they may find comfort on the upper stories — Heaven and Humanity — they cannot remain there indefinitely.

But the people of ancient India loathed the thought of this endless cycle that implied an unstable, ephemeral world and longed to rid themselves of the influence of karma that bound them to the mundane world. They sought a way to escape from the cycle, and Shakyamuni, in expounding the four noble truths and the eightfold path, offered them the promise of an exit. Or, at least, he appeared to do so. What seemed like an exit from transmigration along the six paths was in actuality a door leading to Buddhist truth.

Our world is itself a manifestation of the six paths. To try to escape from it is futile and cannot lead to enlightenment. But this was a matter beyond the understanding of the people, and so, as an expedient, Shakyamuni at first taught that people could escape from the cycle of birth and death by extinguishing both desire and life itself.

Buddhism refined the concept of the six paths, explaining

that they exist not only as external worlds but also as internal states. For example, Animality represents on the one hand animals or their world and, at the same time, the condition of life in which we humans are motivated solely by instinctive desires. Summarizing this view of the six paths, the thirteenth-century Japanese Buddhist master Nichiren, of whom much more will be said later, wrote:

> When we look from time to time at a person's face, we find him or her sometimes joyful, sometimes enraged, and sometimes calm. At times greed appears in the person's face, at times foolishness, and at times perversity. Rage is the world of hell, greed is that of hungry spirits, foolishness is that of animals, perversity is that of asuras, joy is that of heaven, and calmness is that of human beings. [1]

As long as we dwell among the six paths, we are largely controlled by the changing circumstances of our environment. If, while transmigrating among the six paths, we can achieve the requisite wisdom and insight to comprehend the true nature of our lives, however, we can manifest the life of Buddhahood — the supreme jewel in the depths of our being. To do this we have to make strenuous efforts to gain access to a higher condition of life, one that transcends the six lower worlds. Buddhism identifies three further worlds between the six lower ones and the condition of Buddhahood: the worlds of voice-hearers (Learning), cause-awakened ones (Realization) and bodhisattvas.

The state of Learning is a condition in which, through learning and study, we awaken to the impermanence of all things. The state of Realization is a condition in which we perceive the impermanence of all things through our own observation of natural phenomena, such as the fading and shriveling of flowers or fallen leaves. The state of Bodhisattva is a condition in which, through compassion, we devote ourselves to helping others, performing altruistic actions on their behalf. Concerning these three conditions, Nichiren wrote:

> The fact that all things in this world are transient is perfectly clear to us. Is this not because the worlds of the two vehicles [Learning and Realization] are present in the human world? Even a heartless villain loves his wife and children. He too has a portion of the bodhisattva world within him. [2]

The Tenth World

If we add the three higher states of life to the lower six we have, obviously, nine different conditions, ranging from Hell to Bodhisattva. Together, these are called the nine worlds, and they constitute the varying conditions of common mortals. Beyond these nine, which are innate in all common mortals, lies the highest state of life, which embodies the four enlightened virtues — eternity, happiness, true self and purity. This is Buddhahood, a state that exists only as a potential in people's lives unless they develop it through the practice of Buddhism. When we manifest this great potential, the nine life-states of common mortals are not extinguished, as traditionally thought; instead, all fall under the influence of Buddhahood. In this way the nine states all contribute simultaneously, in their various ways, to the construction of happiness for ourselves and others.

Buddhahood, in short, is the condition of absolute and indestructible happiness. "Normal" happiness, by contrast, is only relative happiness. Wealth instead of poverty, health instead of sickness, and peace instead of conflict are all examples of relative happiness — happiness that depends on necessary conditions.

The moment one of these conditions disappears, our happiness is shattered; and, if the loss is a serious one, we experience despair. So, no matter how fully we may be endowed with wealth, financial security, a happy family and a good job, such happiness can in no way be regarded as everlasting. Moreover, even the fact that we are well off in this sense, because it is subject to comparison with the conditions of others, can be a cause of envy or jealousy and so in itself leads to unhappiness. Such finiteness and uncertainty are inherent in mundane happiness and characterize life in this world.

The absolute happiness of Buddhahood, however, is unaffected by circumstantial changes or difficulties. Although absolute happiness does not imply freedom from sufferings and problems, it does indicate possession of a vibrant, sturdy life force and the abundant wisdom to challenge and overcome all sufferings and difficulties we may encounter. By making such a condition our own, we can live with unassailable confidence. Buddhahood is also characterized by deep compassion for others and boundless wisdom. Indeed, all of the elements that enable us to lead truly humane lives are contained in the state of Buddhahood.

To reveal and embody such a supreme state of life is called "attaining" Buddhahood, the ultimate goal of Buddhist practice. Even so, aiming solely at our own enlightenment is not in accord with either the way or spirit of Buddhism. Mahayana Buddhism expounds the importance of teaching and encouraging other people to seek enlightenment and of devoting ourselves, in unity with others, to Buddhist practice — that is, we should practice both for ourselves and for others. These two facets of Buddhist practice are each as necessary to the other as are the two wings of a bird. Efforts to improve society and the environment, therefore, derive naturally from our internal efforts to attain Buddhahood. In the Buddhist view, life and its environment are fundamentally one, or inseparable. Thus, as Buddhists try to attain their own individual enlightenment, they also continually strive to bring peace and prosperity to their respective societies and countries — indeed, to the entire world. To establish lasting global peace and prosperity is the underlying purpose behind the spreading of Buddhism through-out society.

Manifesting one's inherent Buddha nature, then, provides the fundamental solution not only to the four universal suffer-ings — birth, aging, sickness and death — but also, more broadly, to all other sufferings, too.

Nichiren's Approach to Religion

In thirteenth-century Japan, Nichiren promulgated these ideas, which are today practiced by millions of people in nearly two hundred nations. Yet despite this widespread following, many people still know little or nothing of Nichiren's teachings.

Nichiren's teachings have also been misapplied and even exploited in the past as in the case of Japan's militarist author-ities, who branded them as ultranationalistic and superpatriotic. Today, some characterize Nichiren's teachings as exclusivist and sectarian. In fact, nothing could be further from the truth.

Nichiren lived during a period of social upheaval. Natural disasters, epidemics, famine and the threat of foreign invasion terrified the people of Japan. Nichiren was adamant that such trouble had befallen the country because Buddhist teachers of his day neither understood nor taught the significance of the Lotus Sutra. He wrote several discourses and letters explaining his views, and he vigorously criticized the government and other Buddhist teachers, arousing such animosity that he was banished twice.

Any religion will assert the absolute correctness of its teachings. For precisely this reason, religion can easily lead people astray. In full recognition of this, Nichiren struggled to refute the aspects of religion that keep people from entering the path to full awakening, without attacking the followers of specific Buddhist schools or merely trying to expand his own school.

Nichiren's criticism of these aspects is summed up as the four dictums, which point out four unbalanced religious archetypes, and which represent a reasoned religious criticism that strictly identifies sources of self-righteousness and religious authoritarianism. Religion becomes unbalanced, Nichiren taught, through dogmatic emphasis of any of the following concepts:

✦ seeking salvation only through the external power of an absolute being

✦ seeking enlightenment only through direct perception of one's own mind and contentment with this self-enlightenment

✦ benefitting in this life through occult means

✦ allowing oneself to be controlled by precepts or standards

The perfectly balanced teaching succumbs to none of these extremes. Rather, it expounds the fusion of internal and external power as the means to transform the life of the individual as well as the surrounding circumstances. A fully developed religion, as conceived by Nichiren, is completely balanced, harmoniously incorporating the religion's fundamental characteristics without bias or distortion.

The modern significance of Nichiren's four dictums lies not in simply refuting Japanese Buddhist schools but in fully developing the positive power of human life. His teaching transcends the narrow boundaries of a single school. It is a religion for all humanity.

Nam-myoho-renge-kyo

Nichiren wrote:

> The four faces [of the treasure tower] represent the four sufferings of birth, aging, sickness and death. These four aspects of life dignify the tower of our individual lives. By chanting Nam-myoho-renge-kyo through birth, aging, sickness and death, the fragrances of the four virtues [eternity, happiness, true self and purity] are made to issue forth [from our lives]. [3]

The treasure tower, an image that appears in the Lotus Sutra, is a huge tower adorned with seven kinds of treasures. It represents the solemn dignity of human life and symbolizes the lives of those who manifest their inherent Buddhahood. As Nichiren taught, by chanting Nam-myoho-renge-kyo we can transform the four sufferings into the four virtues emanating from the depths of our being.

Nam-myoho-renge-kyo, as we shall explore later, indicates the ultimate Law of life and the universe and hence constitutes the cause for all beings to become enlightened. More specifically, *nam* is an expression of devotion, and *Myoho-renge-kyo*, the title of the Lotus Sutra, is used as a name for the ultimate reality. Nichiren interpreted the Lotus Sutra, in its entirety, as a clarification of Nam-myoho-renge-kyo.

This unique sutra refutes the idea that Shakyamuni first attained enlightenment as Siddhartha in India in the sixth century B.C.E., revealing instead that he had actually been the

Buddha since the inconceivably remote past. This teaching points to the truth that Buddhahood has existed eternally in the lives of all people. In other words, to attain Buddhahood does not require us to become extraordinary beings but merely to strive to manifest our inherent Buddha nature.

Buddhism's ultimate purpose is to enable all human beings to realize the true nature of life. This truth, although alluded to in many sutras, cannot be fully revealed in words. Shakyamuni himself realized it not through words but by devoting himself to many kinds of practice and finally by engaging in meditation under what is now called the bodhi (or bo) tree. Even before he attained enlightenment, however, both the ultimate truth and the wisdom to perceive it were present within his life. What Shakyamuni did was to bring them forth, thereby breaking free from the fetters of desire and illusion. He found it impossible, however, to convey this truth to other people completely through the medium of words. So, as he expounded his teachings, Shakyamuni helped his disciples fully understand them by prescribing various types of practice. Likewise, we today can attain enlightenment only by assiduously devoting ourselves to Buddhist practice. For this reason, both practice and study are equally indispensable. It is impossible to attain enlightenment either by practicing meditation alone or by studying the Buddhist teachings alone — both are necessary.

In the Lotus Sutra, Shakyamuni expounded the ultimate truth of life. Although he used thousands of words to describe it, however, no single word or phrase can clearly define it. Shakyamuni expected that his disciples and future followers would realize this truth through devotion to practices he had prescribed. Such practices require tremendous patience and effort, which in turn demand that one place complete belief and trust in the Buddha and in his teachings. But to follow this path involves renunciation of secular life and the devotion of all one's time to Buddhist practice. For this reason, for centuries the only people who could fully engage themselves in Buddhist practice were monks, priests and nuns. Lay believers supported them financially and materially, thereby accumulating much good karma for themselves, but generally they did not hope to attain enlightenment in their present existence.

Nichiren crystallized in universally accessible form the ultimate truth expounded in the Lotus Sutra, in effect opening the way for all people to attain enlightenment, or Buddhahood. He made this possible by clarifying in words the ultimate truth of life — the Law of Nam-myoho-renge-kyo. This phrase incorporates the two essential aspects of Buddhism: the truth itself and the practice to develop the wisdom to realize that truth. Nichiren taught his followers to believe in the truth expressed by Nam-myoho-renge-kyo and to chant the phrase. Nam-myoho-renge-kyo thus represents the goal of practice — and the goal of Shakyamuni and all the other Buddhas as well — and at the same time it is the means of achieving that goal.

It is my conviction that Shakyamuni and Nichiren were both enlightened to the same truth, and that their teachings differed only because of differences in their time periods, their audiences, the cultures in which they operated and other elements. Their enlightenment is truly universal in that all humanity can share in it through carrying out correct Buddhist practice. Suffice it to say that Nichiren's teachings contain the essence of all the teachings of Buddhism. These various teachings, however, were first expounded by Shakyamuni and later expanded upon by his successors. For this reason, in this book I refer to the teachings of Shakyamuni, Nichiren, Nagarjuna, T'ien-t'ai and other Buddhist scholars.

The significance of Buddhism lies both in the discovery of

the Buddha nature in all beings and in the establishment of a practical method for bringing it out, so that human beings can derive maximum meaning from their lives. This reformation of the inner human world — what we in the Soka Gakkai International call *human revolution* — is especially relevant to modern civilization, which has long been trapped in a sort of spiritual quicksand. We can escape the quicksand by calling forth the supreme human potential available to each of us.

Through examining life from the viewpoint of Buddhism, I believe we can grasp the true nature of the fundamental problems of existence and see for ourselves the way to solving them.

CHAPTER ONE

Birth

A MERCIFUL RAIN falls everywhere, equally, mois-
tening the earth's vast expanse and bringing forth
new life from all the trees and grasses, large and small. This com-
pelling image from the Lotus Sutra, depicted with the sutra's
characteristic vividness, grandeur and beauty, symbolizes the
awakening of all people touched by the Buddha's Law. At the
same time, it is a magnificent tribute to the rich diversity of
human and all other life, sentient and insentient. Each living
thing manifests its Buddha nature; each contributes its harmony
to the grand concert of symbiosis.

The Buddhist term *dependent origination* describes this symbiotic nature of life. As Goethe, speaking through Faust, wrote,
"Into the whole, how all things blend, each in the other working, living,"[1] Buddhism explains that nothing and no one exist
in isolation. Each individual entity shapes its environment,
which affects all other existences. All things are mutually supportive and interrelated, forming a living cosmos, what modern philosophy might call a semantic whole. This is the
conceptual framework through which Mahayana Buddhism
views life and the natural universe.

Consider the concept of causation. When viewed in terms of
dependent origination, causal relationships differ fundamentally

from the mechanistic idea of cause and effect that, according to modern science, holds sway over the natural world. The scientific model often seems divorced from subjective human concerns. When an accident or disaster takes place, mechanistic causation can identify how it occurred. It is silent, however, on why certain individuals and not others should be caught up in the tragic event. Indeed, the mechanistic view requires the deliberate dismissal of existential questions.

In contrast, the more broadly defined Buddhist understanding of causation takes into account human existence and directly addresses poignant uncertainties. In the early formulation of Shakyamuni's teachings, the following exchange is said to have occurred: "'What is the cause of aging and death?' 'Birth is the cause of aging and death.'"[2] This emphasis on relatedness and interdependence may seem to suggest that individual identity is nullified or obscured. But Buddhist scripture addresses this in a passage that reads: "You are your own master. Could anyone else be your master? When you have gained control over yourself, you have found a master of rare value."[3] Another passage records Shakyamuni's putative last words as: "Be lamps unto yourselves. Be a refuge unto yourselves. Rely on yourselves. Hold fast to the Law as a lamp, do not rely on anything else."[4]

Both passages urge us to live independently and true to ourselves. The self referred to here, however, is not the "lesser self" caught up in the snares of egoism. Rather, it is the "greater self" in harmony with the life of the universe through which cause and effect are interlocked over the infinite reaches of space and time.

Similar to the unifying and integrating self that Carl Jung perceived in the depths of the ego, the term *greater self* in Buddhism expresses the openness and expansiveness of character by which we can embrace all people's sufferings as our own. The greater self always seeks to alleviate pain and to augment the happiness of others here amid the realities of everyday life. Furthermore, the dynamic, vital awakening of the greater self enables each individual to experience both life and death with equal delight.

The Significance of the Treasure Tower

Nichiren wrote: "We adorn the treasure tower of our being with the four aspects [of birth, aging, sickness and death]."[5] The treasure tower referred to here is first mentioned in the eleventh chapter of the Lotus Sutra, "The Emergence of the Treasure Tower." That chapter as a whole can be interpreted as a metaphor for birth and human life. The text describes a massive tower emerging from the earth and hovering in mid-air. It stands at the center of the universe, and its immense size represents how the life of each person is as vast as the universe. The tower is adorned with seven kinds of treasure — gold, silver, lapis lazuli, seashell, agate, pearl and carnelian — indicating that each person's life is a cluster of jewels. Seated inside the tower is Many Treasures Buddha, who comes from the world of Treasure Purity.

Though interpretations of the significance of the treasure tower vary widely, Nichiren explained that it "refers to our individual bodies."[6] Likening the appearance of the treasure tower to one's emergence in birth, he wrote, "The Treasure Purity world is the mother's womb,"[7] and, "the process of emerging from this womb is called 'coming forth and appearing.'"[8]

The world of Treasure Purity denotes neither some special land nor an idealistic world. As no treasure is more valuable than life, the mother's womb, in which life takes form and from which it is born, is itself this most sacred Treasure Purity world.

The treasure tower illustrates that our lives and the universe are one. Yet this profound truth often eludes us. To realize it means to see ourselves as the treasure tower, or to awaken our Buddha nature.

What Causes Life?

Even with the poetic metaphor of the treasure tower, we are still left to question: Where does life come from? What causes it?

Since ancient times, human beings have been fascinated by the mystery of life's origin, by questions of why we are here on earth just as we are and what has caused us to be this way. In our quest, we have stretched the limits of our spirits, plumbed the depths of our minds, and conducted endless laboratory experiments. All this work has yielded no definitive answers but rather an assortment of religious and philosophical hypotheses.

Buddhism views the universe as one life entity. The universe is imbued with life, and wherever conditions are right, life will emerge.

In the most conventional sense, of course, we are born from the union of our mothers and fathers. At the joining together of the spermatozoon and the ovum, an embryo is formed. As the embryo develops, so do the various functions of body and mind.

Something about the development of a new life, however, cannot be explained simply by the spermatozoon and ovum union. The embryo's development based on the genetic information it has received and the environmental influences it experiences cannot be ascribed merely to chemical reactions. Something much more profound must cause life to emerge.

Buddhism explains that there are four stages of life: existence during birth, existence during life, existence during death and the existence during the period between death and rebirth, or the intermediate existence or stage. Life is understood to repeat the cycle of these four stages eternally.

Birth, like death, is a process. Some sutras describe conception as the appearance of an entity of intermediate existence, or the introduction of consciousness. Conception is the moment when this intermediate existence is wedded to its new human form.

Life in all its forms and at all times contains the urge to create, is inherently active, and possesses the positive power of self-generation. Indeed, life is a grand and eternal pulse that constantly seeks to become manifest throughout the universe whenever conditions are right. The power and functions that work within life to promote its self-manifestation can be called "internal causes." Buddhism tells us that internal causes (including, as we shall see, the karma carried through the intermediate stage) interact with external causes to bring about the circumstances and conditions of birth.

Western science generally considers the spermatozoon and ovum the sole essentials for conception, maintaining that only fertilization of the female gamete is a necessary prerequisite. By contrast, the Buddhist view is that not only the spermatozoon and ovum but also life itself—in the state of intermediate existence and with karma that matches the conditions of conception, heredity, family and social conditions into which the life will be born—are each necessary for human life to come into being and develop. Conception results from the union of all three.

To illustrate, a couple has intercourse and fertilization is about to take place. Due to the combination of DNA from both parents, their potential child will inherit the genes for a birth defect. Conception cannot take place, however, without the "availability" of a life entity in the intermediate stage of existence that has made the causes to experience the effects of being born with and suffering from that birth defect. The life and karma of the mother, father and child—all must align.

Destiny, Heredity and Environment

How is it that children can take after their parents and yet differ in both character and appearance from all the other members of their family?

Gregor Mendel partially answered this question in the 1860s when he proposed the basic laws of heredity, which were then widely ignored. Further studies in genetics have led scientists to believe that genes play the central role in the inheritance of traits, enabling hereditary information to be passed from parent to child at the moment of fertilization, as male and female gametes fuse.

Is our character the result of heredity or of environment? This is a difficult question, shrouded in controversy. Perhaps it cannot really be decided. Today, many believe that genes largely dictate one's nature. Yet, obviously, character is so complex that it cannot be entirely determined by heredity.

Two major theories address the shaping of character: the inborn, which emphasizes hereditary factors, and the empirical, which stresses environmental influences—views generally known as "nature" and "nurture." One's character is likely formed by the interaction of both. Moreover, human beings—unlike animals, whose behavior is largely instinctual—can initiate action, another character-shaping factor that must be taken into account.

Whatever the case, although we are all born into this world in similar fashion, no two of us develop in exactly the same way or in exactly the same circumstances. Some are born rich, others poor, some clever and others not so. Why such widely varying circumstances and diverse destinies? Buddhism gives a clear-cut answer based firmly on the law of cause and effect. As one sutra states: "If you want to understand the causes that existed in the past, look at the results as they appear in the present. And if you want to understand what results will appear in the future, look at the causes that exist in the present."[9] Rather than focusing on the past, Buddhism emphasizes the present and future. We are encouraged to face reality no matter how tough it may be, and to realize that by our actions from this point on, we can alter the influence of our past causes.

Understandably, we may wish to ascribe everything to hereditary and environmental factors not of our own making. Ultimately, however, it is only our determined, constant efforts to improve ourselves, to tap our innate capacity to reach beyond inner limitations that will empower us to enjoy the full range of our abilities and achieve what otherwise we could hardly conceive.

The Buddhist View of Transmigration

Since the beginning of history, people have sensed the presence of some spiritual force, the continued existence of which lies at the core of all things. In India, the concept of transmigration — the passing of an individual's essence from one life to the next — has been accepted since very early times. Ancient Greeks, too, believed that something continues on after an individual's death, something that undergoes a continual cycle of birth and death. In about the seventh century B.C.E., a religion called Orphism advocated purification of the soul achieved through a cycle of reincarnation. Later, around the fifth century B.C.E, the Pythagoreans advanced the concept of metempsychosis, or the transmigration of the soul.

Buddhism teaches instead that what transmigrates is *karma*. Karma is a grammatical variation of the Sanskrit *karman*, which means act or action. Karma refers to potentials in the inner, unconscious realm of life created through one's actions in the past or present, which, respectively, after being activated by external stimuli, manifest as results in the present or future.

Sometimes the manifest effects are positive, what we might consider rewards; and sometimes they are negative, what we might term as retribution. As we will discuss further in chapter four, potentials that do not come to fruition continue to exist even after we die. They will accompany one into the next life-time and so on until encountering the external cause that will bring forth the effect of the potential.

According to Buddhism, life takes on no physical entity after death, nor does a "spirit" or "soul" continue to exist as a fixed entity. There is no fixed self that lives on as an unchanging entity. Shakyamuni concluded that it is karma itself that continues. Our circumstances in this present lifetime are the effect of our past actions (karma), and our actions in the present determine the circumstances of our lives in the future. In other words, the influence of our actions carries on from one existence to the next, transcending the life and death of the human being.

The Meaning of Karma

Each of us creates our own karma. Our past thoughts, speech and behavior have shaped our present reality, and our actions (and thoughts and speech) in the present will in turn affect our future. The influence of karma carries over from one lifetime to the next, remaining through the latent state between death and rebirth. The law of karma accounts for the circumstances of one's birth, one's individual nature and the differences among all living beings and their environments.

The idea of karma predates Buddhism and had already permeated Indian society well before Shakyamuni's time. The pre-Buddhist view of karma, however, contained an element of determinism. It served more to explain people's lot in life and to compel them to accept it rather than inspire hope for change or transformation.

Buddhist teachings further developed the idea of karma. Shakyamuni maintained that what makes a person noble or humble is not birth but actions taken. Therefore, the Buddhist doctrine of karma is not fatalistic. Karma is viewed not only as a means to explain the present but also as the potential force through which to influence our future.

Good karma, then, means actions born from good intentions, kindness and compassion. Conversely, bad karma refers to actions induced by greed, anger and foolishness (or the holding of mistaken views). Some Buddhist treatises divide the causes of bad karma into ten acts: the three physical acts of killing, stealing and sexual misconduct; the four verbal acts of lying, flattery (or idle and irresponsible speech), defamation and duplicity; and the three mental acts of greed, anger and foolishness.

Buddhism teaches that the chain of cause and effect exists eternally; this accounts for the influence of karma amassed in prior lifetimes. The influence of such karma resides within the depths of our lives and, when activated by the moment-to-moment realities of this lifetime, shapes our lives according to its dictates. Some karmic effects may appear in this lifetime while others may remain dormant. "Fixed karma" produces a fixed result at a specific time, whereas the result of "unfixed karma," of course, is neither fixed nor set to appear at a predetermined time.

Some karma is so heavy, so profoundly imprinted in the depths of people's lives, that it cannot easily be altered. For instance, suppose someone deliberately makes another person extremely unhappy or even causes that person's death; whether the guilty party escapes apparent accountability or is arrested and dealt with according to judicial procedures, either way, that person has created heavy negative karma. According to the strict law of causality, this negative karma will surely lead to karmic suffering far beyond one's ordinary powers to eradicate it. Such grave karma usually exerts its influence at death, and the most influential karma at the time of death will determine one's basic life-condition in the next lifetime.

The influence of particular karma will be extinguished after its energy is unleashed in one's life. This is similar to a plant seed that sprouts and grows to blossom as a flower or bear fruit. After fulfilling its function, the same seed will never repeat the process.

Bad karma can be erased only after it "blossoms" in the form of our suffering. According to pre-Lotus Sutra teachings, the influence of severely bad karma, created through numerous actions, could only be erased through several lifetimes; and one could attain Buddhahood only by accumulating good causes in lifetime after lifetime. But the Lotus Sutra teaches that the principal cause for attaining Buddhahood is the Buddha nature inherent in each individual life, and that faith in the Lotus Sutra opens the way to that attainment. It is not required that we undergo lifetime after lifetime of austerities. Through our diligent practice of faith in the Lotus Sutra, we can instantly tap our innate Buddhahood and extricate ourselves from the effects of our bad karma in this lifetime. Moreover, the transformation of an individual's life-condition can evoke a similar transformation in others. As this process ripples outward, similar transformations become possible throughout entire societies, all humankind and even into the natural world.

Karma and Medical Technology

By changing our genes, can we change our karma? This, too, is a difficult question. While it may be possible to overcome a particular illness by genetic alteration, thereby technically solving our problem, this will not, according to Buddhism, change the influence of our karma. Without changing our life-condition on the deepest level, we are destined to experience the anguish resulting from whatever causes we have made in the past.

In keeping with Buddhism's regard for the sacredness of life, we must demonstrate extreme caution in applying technologies capable of manipulating life itself. If genetic therapy can provide solutions for certain problems, it should be considered as an option, but first it must be carefully and seriously examined. All possible precautions must be taken to prevent therapy from degenerating into the genetic manipulation of people for non-therapeutic ends.

With regard to genetic "defects," distinguishing the normal from the pathological is not easy. Many who suffer from genetically transmitted defects or severe illnesses consider their lives happy and worth living. In defining quality of life, we must not draw boundaries and designate everything beyond those boundaries as unlivable. Instead we must do everything in our power to build a broad-minded society in which people with disabilities do not have to consider themselves handicapped and can realize their full potential.

No one would dispute that humanity has benefited greatly from the discoveries of medical science. For example, thanks to modern medicine, fetuses come successfully to term that until recently would have certainly miscarried. Also, prenatal tests allow us to monitor the very early stages of fetal development and identify a growing number of congenital and hereditary disorders.

Recent technological progress, however, which has been made at a dizzying speed, raises ethical questions. For example, if a congenital deformity is detected, the decision whether to carry the fetus to term is often left to the parents. Providing equipment for prenatal testing is important, but we must also create a social system that can support and advise parents in such situations.

Medicine treats the relatively superficial causes of life's miseries. Ultimately, causes of health problems lie far beyond the realm of medicine, in the area identified by Buddhism as karma. Buddhism pursues these profound, ultimate causes so that a secure and happy future can be assured.

In other words, while medical science pursues health, Buddhism seeks the purpose for which people are born into this world, thus enabling them to lead lives of the highest possible value. The Lotus Sutra defines *this world* as the place where "living beings enjoy themselves at ease." To be born on this earth and to enjoy every instant of living until the last possible moment—this is the purpose of practicing Buddhism.

The Oneness of Life and the Environment

Nichiren once wrote: "Environment is like the shadow, and life, the body. Without the body, no shadow can exist, and without life, no environment. In the same way, life is shaped by its environment."[10]

The environment and the living body are seemingly separate phenomena that mutually influence each other, yet both are, in essence, embodiments of the ultimate reality of life. They are "two but not two," or essentially one. Buddhism refers to this principle as the oneness of life and its environment.

The significance of this oneness principle lies in the fact that, rather than being at the mercy of our turbulent and ever-changing environment, we human beings can instead infuence our environment from the inside out. As we cultivate our Buddha nature, our actions increasingly accord with our deepest wisdom and compassion. As we become indestructibly happy, that happiness is echoed in our environment. This principle urges us to bring forth our innate Buddha nature so solidly that we can build indestructible happiness within us regardless of what adversity or ease our environment presents.

Increasingly, people are seeing the world as made up not just of separate things but of interrelated phenomena, a view that accords with the Buddhist concepts of dependent causation and oneness of life and its environment.

Goethe's unified view of nature, of life phenomena, is also being rediscovered. As he wrote: "The time will inevitably come when mechanistic and atomic thinking will be put out of the minds of all people of wisdom, and instead dynamics and chemistry will come to be seen in all phenomena. When that happens, the divinity of living Nature will unfold before our eyes all the more clearly."[11]

The Universe Is Life

Josei Toda once said:

We use the word *self*, but this word actually refers to the universe. When we ask how the life of the universe is different from the life of each of you, the only differences we

find are those of your bodies and minds. Your life and that
of the universe are the same.

Toda's thesis on the philosophy of life states that the universe
is life itself, and that life, together with the universe, is eternal
and everlasting. He said, "Just as we sleep and wake and then
sleep again, we live and die and then live again, maintaining our
lives eternally." And: "When we wake up in the morning, we
resume our activities based on the same mind as the previous
day. In the same way, in each new existence we are destined to
live based on the result of the karmic causes created in our previous lives."

Toda also explained that if we liken the universe to an ocean,
our lives are like the waves that appear and disappear on the
surface of that ocean — the waves and the ocean are not separate entities. In other words, the waves are but part of the
ocean's ongoing activity.

This is similar to a remark by the twentieth-century British
philosopher Alan Watts: "There is no separate 'you' to get something out of the universe.... As the ocean 'waves' so the universe 'peoples'.... What we therefore see as 'death,' empty space
or nothingness is only the trough between the crests of this endless waving ocean of life."[12]

Toda described life as the very basis of all things, which we
perceive as changing and flowing. However, he said, the true
nature of life is actually neither flowing nor still; it is like empty
space. It is an entity that is simultaneously the infinite macrocosm as well as each of the microcosms of countless living
beings. It is an enormous life-entity always undergoing dynamic
change and, at the same time, eternal and everlasting. The Mystic Law is the name we give to this undeniable, sublime entity
— universal life — of which we are all embodiments.

Looking Ahead

The very fact that we have been born as human beings indicates our potential to alter the course of our lives. Therefore, when the influence of our karma results in an obstacle or hardship, this is actually a splendid opportunity to improve our state of life. By recognizing that the present obstacle indicates the fulfillment and therefore the termination of a potential that had already been created, we can fill our lives instead with the influence of good karma from this point on. With confidence in this idea, we can, through practicing Buddhist principles, take advantage of every seeming misfortune as a chance to grow.

As we awaken to our power to overcome all obstacles, we will invite a great future for ourselves and in the process develop a much more powerful state of life. We can free our lives in order to discover our true purpose and become happy, and we can contribute to improving our society and even the entire world.

Discovering life's purpose plays a vital role in facing the second of the four sufferings—aging—which we will examine in the next chapter.

CHAPTER TWO

Aging

THAT CHANGE is the essential nature of reality is certainly not a new concept. As far back as the sixth century B.C.E, the Greek philosopher Heraclitus declared that all things are in a state of flux, and that you cannot step into the same river twice. Indeed, everything, whether in the realm of natural phenomena or of human affairs, changes continuously. Nothing maintains exactly the same state for even the briefest instant; the most solid-seeming rocks and minerals are subject to the erosive effects of time.

The Transience of All Phenomena

Buddhism calls this ephemeral aspect of reality "the transience of all phenomena." In Buddhist cosmology, this concept is described as the repeated cycles of formation, continuance, decline and disintegration through which all systems must pass, including each of us. No matter what we do, human life keeps changing. Buddhism teaches that all phenomena are impermanent, including our own bodies.

Despite the inevitability of aging, we often refuse to reconcile ourselves to the fact that we are growing older every single second. In the past, the elderly were treated with great respect as they imparted knowledge and tradition to the community. Today, with speed and efficiency valued above tradition, the elderly are largely excluded from mainstream society. Often they are viewed more as burdens than assets. It is hardly surprising that people resent growing old and do everything in their power to slow the aging process.

Medical science has studied the human aging phenomenon from various angles. Some say life span is determined by the limits of cell division. Others claim that aging is genetically controlled. Regardless of *why* we age, it is vital that we face aging without fear; that we look at how to live and age with dignity.

Nichiren wrote of the preciousness of life, declaring that an extra day is worth more than ten million ounces of gold.[1] If one more day of living is worth a fortune, how important it is, then, that we recognize the sanctity of life—once a life is lost, it can never be recovered. With this recognition, however, the point is not just to cling to life as long as possible; it's making each day of life count.

Nichiren also wrote: "Life as a human being is hard to sustain—as hard as it is for the dew to remain on the grass. But it is better to live a single day with honor than to live to 120 and die in disgrace."[2] Our challenge is to make each day meaningful, to be concerned more with *how* we live than how *long*.

Eternity and Impermanence

In the last chapter, we discussed the idea that life is eternal. At the same time, human life, like all phenomena, is impermanent. These two truths ultimately complement rather than contradict each other.

So great are the psychological and physical changes as a person grows from infancy to maturity that the entire person seems transformed. Yet throughout the process, there is a "self" that unites mind and body and remains relatively constant. In Buddhism, this is called the "greater self."

At any given time, we can be either engaged compassionately with or withdrawn from our environment. When open and engaged, we are experiencing the greater self. When closed off, we are putting forth our "lesser self." The lesser self is a deluded condition, while the greater self is synonymous with the Buddha nature. To live for the greater self means to recognize the universal principle behind all things and, thus awakened, rise above the suffering caused by awareness of impermanence. A belief in something eternal is needed to enhance our quality of existence. By believing this lifetime is the be-all and end-all of existence, we will miss out on living a truly profound life.

We might think of it this way: While young children may enjoy splashing about in plastic wading pools, they will grow dissatisfied upon discovering the fun of real swimming pools. But even an Olympic-sized pool may prove unsatisfactory after they enjoy a swim in the vast ocean.

Similarly, when our viewpoint expands beyond the boundaries of our present existence to include the entire, eternal universe, we can live deeply fulfilling lives.

The Problems of Aging

We can address the problems of aging from several angles, including the biological, psychological and sociological. Biologists and physicians work to counter or even eliminate degenerative diseases, aiming to extend the healthy human life span well beyond the centenarian. Psychologists attempt to alleviate the wide variety of depressive illnesses that commonly afflict the elderly. Social gerontologists work to make old age as comfortable and pleasant as possible. For these endeavors to be fully effective, however, they must be carried out in conjunction with one another. Although the biological, psychological and social symptoms of aging appear separately, there is generally an interaction among them. Therefore, to find solutions to the many problems of aging, we need the cooperation of scientists from various disciplines.

There are many differences among people at any particular age but especially when they are older. We are far more alike at seven months old than at seventy years. That's because although aging is an inescapable process, the rate of aging varies widely from person to person. Hence, some adults look younger than their age and others look older.

In 1970, I formed a group with some friends who were all born the same year as I, 1928. Every time we meet, I notice afresh that those whose eyes shine look younger than they are. This indicates two things. First, the calendar is not the ultimate measure of a person's age: physiological, psychological and spiritual factors all play their parts. Second, the shining eyes of an elderly person indicate strength that is spiritual, which, in turn, enhances one's physical vitality.

As we grow older, our internal organs slowly atrophy and our joints become less supple. But these are not serious problems in themselves. Even in old age, we possess the inherent life force to repair the injured parts of our bodies. And there is no reason, even in old age, not to exercise in order to maintain physical well-being. If we suffer a serious illness in our later years, we may be tempted to avoid using our bodies and minds as actively as before, even after we recover; but this only weakens us. We need not restrict our activities simply because the years are ticking by.

To combat the sufferings of aging, then, we need to acquire

wisdom. Wisdom allows us to ensure our well-being. Awareness of how to prevent illness before it occurs and how to preserve our health is necessary so that we can go about our activities with zest and energy. Rather than succumbing passively to old age, we should engage it head-on, positively and actively. The field of health science offers us a special type of wisdom that teaches us how to accomplish that.

Two significant factors account for much of what we describe loosely as the aging process: biological changes related to the aging of the brain and other parts of the body, such as the autonomic nervous system, the endocrine system and the circulatory system; and social customs and institutions, such as the mandatory retirement age, that may change the lifestyle and mindset of those growing older. As mentioned, biological changes can be coped with. From a social viewpoint, we must concentrate both on what we can do for the elderly and on what they can do for themselves.

Attitudes About Aging

None of us is immune to old age.

Shakyamuni once spoke of the need to conquer three forms of pride—pride of youth, of health and of life. Drunk with the pride of youth, people have an aversion to those bent with age. Drunk with the pride of health, people have an aversion to those suffering from illness or disease. And drunk with the pride of life, people have an aversion to the dead. But by looking away from the realities of aging, sickness and death, we deny our own future; we reject our inevitable fate.

A psychologist has defined the three problems of old age as anxiety, loneliness and a sense of uselessness. A sociologist has said that they are poverty, sickness and loneliness. Though some day society may eliminate poverty and disease, feelings of lone-liness, uselessness and anxiety are much more difficult to tackle.

Nichiren wrote of a place called "The Country Where Old People Were Abandoned." It is described in Buddhist scripture as a land where the elderly were discarded, left to die so there would be fewer mouths to feed. Then one day the country was faced with a terrible crisis, only to be saved by the wisdom of one elderly man whose son had hidden him away, refusing to follow custom. The king thereupon changed the laws to ensure that the elderly would be treated with reverence.

The rich life experiences of older people constitute a precious and irreplaceable resource. It behooves us, then, to pay atten-tion to the way we view aging and to create a society in which the elderly can experience fulfillment and live out their lives as they wish. This, indeed, should be the ideal of the science of gerontology.

It is terrible when the aged, who most likely grew old during long years of service to their families and to society, feel cut off from that very society. Often, they respond by closing their minds and isolating themselves. The elderly, aware that they cannot do many things as they once did, understandably find the problems and limitations difficult to accept.

Every society has both a bright and a dark aspect. Through-out history, women, children and the aged have been margin-alized rather than placed in the limelight. Nichiren, recognizing this tendency, wrote appreciatively of King Wen, a wise monarch of ancient China. Wen was aware of the difficulties his country's elderly faced and provided them with as much sup-port as possible, establishing a kind of welfare state. Because of the king's widespread benevolence, wrote Nichiren, the dynasty founded by Wen prospered for thirty-seven successive genera-tions—some eight hundred years.

A culture that values the elderly values humanity. Efforts in both the family and society at large are needed to create a compassionate and spiritually rich culture and, at the same time, to build practical networks to meet the needs of the elderly.

The Brighter Side of Aging

Some years ago, *The New York Times* published an article about research findings by a group of scientists under the headline "The Aging Mind Proves Capable of Lifelong Growth."[3] The article concluded that aging brings about development in some areas of the mind and decline in others. While "fluid intelligence" diminishes, "crystallized intelligence" gradually increases.

Fluid intelligence is defined as "a set of abilities involved in seeing and using abstract relationships and patterns." This flexibility of thinking is used, for example, in playing chess. Crystallized intelligence, on the other hand, means "the ability to use an accumulated body of general information to make judgments and solve problems. In practical terms, crystallized intelligence comes into play in understanding arguments made in newspaper editorials, or dealing with problems for which there are no clear answers, but only better and worse options."[4]

It would appear that there is no scientific basis to suppose that intelligence decreases significantly with age. The article quotes Martha Storandt at Washington University in St. Louis, who said: "The fluid intelligence drop has some impact, but people learn to compensate, even in later life. You can still learn what you want to; it just takes a little longer."[5]

Warner Schaie, an eminent U.S. researcher in aging, added: "For some mental capacities, there begin to be slight declines in the sixties, and, for most people, there are meaningful declines by the eighties. But some mental capacities decline very little, or can even improve in old age. Some of our people have shown no declines that interfere with daily living into their eighties."[6]

A noted American gerontologist, Dr. Belle Boone Beard, spent two decades studying centenarians. She concluded that when people continually make use of their powers of memory and concentration, those abilities do not decline.[7]

The Third Stage of Life

People who have accumulated great wisdom and experience through their efforts in earlier years inspire our confidence. Their insight broadens and deepens as they get older. Accordingly, we would do well to consider the life we are leading, for this will affect the nature of our own old age.

We can look at our school years as our first stage of life and the years after that as our second stage. Our retirement years, when we put the finishing touches on our lives, become the third stage. Though our bodies may weaken, as long as we set our minds to it we can still make our lives shine.

A saying goes: "To a fool, old age is a bitter winter; to a sage, it is a golden time." Depending on their outlook, the old age period will be dramatically different for people, especially in terms of the richness and fulfillment they will experience. Everything is up to our attitude, how we approach life. Do we look at old age as a descending path to oblivion? Or is it a period in which we can attain our goals and bring our lives to a rewarding, satisfying completion? It has been said that aging gracefully is more difficult than dying, but as long as we have a forward-looking, positive attitude, a spirit to take on challenges, we will gain depth in our lives.

There is a world of difference, too, in how we refer to old age, whether we can indeed view it as the third stage of life or whether it is simply our remaining years. While "remaining years" sounds like useless leftovers, "the third stage" emphasizes the shining potential life still holds. Again, to quote Goethe: "Joy of existence is great, / Joy at existence is greater."

A life of purpose and commitment begins with setting goals. In our old age, more than any other time, we must question our worth as human beings. Do we still value something in our hearts besides prestige and social position?

Dr. Norman Cousins, a peace activist and former UCLA School of Medicine adjunct professor, once said to me: "Death is not the greatest tragedy that befalls us in life. What is far more tragic is for an important part of oneself to die while one is still alive. There is no more terrifying tragedy than this. What is important is to accomplish something in life."

The purpose of our lives, to the very last moment, is to achieve something of value. No lives are nobler than those of individuals dedicated to something they believe in and fighting for it wholeheartedly, who give their lives selflessly to their beliefs. When you reach old age, you know in your heart if you are satisfied with your life. No one else can know this or decide it for you. The greatest challenge we face in our rapidly aging society is whether we can say honestly at the end of our days that our lives were well spent.

A positive attitude gives us new energy: "The future awaits me. I have new goals, and I'm going to meet them!" By living each day to the fullest, we can bring our lives to a magnificent close like golden rays at sunset illuminating the sky in all directions.

How then can the elderly maintain a sense of purpose and usefulness of mind? Recent scientific studies have pointed to such factors as:

✦ Staying socially involved. Deterioration is more rapid in older people who withdraw from society.

✦ Being mentally active. Continuing to pursue intellectual interests tends to increase verbal intelligence. Engaging in cognitively stimulating activities and pastimes such as bridge, chess, learning a musical instrument or foreign language helps alter neurological processes, even those involved in the onset of Alzheimer's disease and other forms of dementia.

✦ Having a flexible personality. A long-term study found that those who could tolerate ambiguity and enjoy new experiences the most in middle age maintained their mental alertness best in their later years.

✦ Keeping a sense of humor. Humor is a powerful defense against feelings of powerlessness, the bane of growing older. A positive mental outlook enhanced by a life steeped in laughter can affect the secretion of endorphins. These hormones act upon the mechanisms of pain and inhibit one's emotional response to it, reducing suffering. As Mark Twain put it, "Against the assault of laughter, nothing can stand."

There are many other practical things we can do to create a happy, beneficial old age. For example, getting enough rest; exhaustion is the cause of many illnesses. Attention should also be paid to diet, taking care to ensure that our meals are well balanced and that we avoid overindulging.

According to Nichiren, "If we consider the power of the Lotus Sutra, we will find perpetual youth and eternal life before our eyes."[8] As we age, perpetual youth can be ours in spirit, yet our bodies are neither immortal nor can they remain youthful throughout our lives. This makes it all the more crucial that we lead satisfying lives, making each day count.

Death is inevitable, and so it makes sense to view death positively, as the point of departure for a new life. The first step in acquiring a positive view is to fully realize that life is eternal. While we will explore this topic at some length in chapter four, suffice it to say for now that in Buddhism, eternity is an endless series of moments, and each individual moment contains eternity. Both eternity and the moment exist in our lives. Buddhism's purpose is to enable us to realize this eternity within our present lifetime and live to the fullest.

Buddhism is not merely a theoretical construct; it is a practical philosophy that helps us steer our lives as we actually live them, moment by moment, toward the achievement of happiness and value. The essential ingredient in this sense of self-worth is for us to recognize our greatest inherent treasure — the Buddha nature.

Nichiren taught: "When you concentrate the exertions of one hundred million aeons in a single life-moment, the three bodies of the Buddha will become manifest in your every thought and act."[9]

"Exertions of one hundred million aeons" refers to the ability to confront each of life's problems with our full being, awakening the total consciousness and leaving no inner resource untapped. By wholeheartedly and directly meeting life's challenges, we bring forth from within ourselves the "three bodies of the Buddha," which are truth, wisdom and compassion. The light of this internal wisdom constantly encourages and guides us toward true and correct action.

The eternal state of Buddhahood wells up within those who practice the Lotus Sutra. And in accord with the plea in the sutra, "Let us live out our lives,"[10] our life force is strengthened

THREE BODIES OF A BUDDHA

Originally meant three types of Buddhas or three ways that a Buddha manifests. The sixth century Buddhist teacher T'ien-t'ai taught that they represent three integral aspects of a single Buddha.

1. The **DHARMA BODY** indicates the essential property of a Buddha, which is the truth or Law to which the Buddha is enlightened.

2. The **REWARD BODY** indicates the wisdom, or the spiritual property of a Buddha, which enables the Buddha to perceive the truth. It is called reward body because a Buddha's wisdom is considered the reward derived from ceaseless effort and discipline.

3. The **MANIFESTED BODY** indicates compassionate actions, or the physical property of a Buddha. It is the body with which a Buddha carries out compassionate actions to lead people to enlightenment.

and our lives extended as a result of our practice and desire to lead others to happiness. When we act on that desire, we are living the Buddhist ideal of the bodhisattva. Bodhisattvas do not strive to live long solely for their own sakes. They do so to serve others to the greatest possible extent, using their experience, their seamless blend of compassion and wisdom, to do so. This is a subtle but crucial difference.

Nichiren wrote of a great bodhisattva, calling him "the old man who is Bodhisattva Superior Practices"[11] and implying by the expression "old man" a venerable, majestic greatness. It brings to mind the virtues of one who has gained true mastery of life—qualities such as firm, unwavering faith; ceaseless, compassionate action; indomitable courage; gripping conversation;

unflagging patience; transcendent nobility and dignity; and a vast, inexhaustible reservoir of wisdom.

Looking Ahead

Even when we are old, we think we will somehow live on. We refuse to recognize that we are in a state of physical decline and could die at any moment. It sounds terrible—no wonder we resist the thought. But understanding the full meaning of aging and death is probably our most significant challenge. If we do not fully understand the nature of our lives — the fleeting aspect as well as the eternal—we can neither live meaningfully nor die in peace.

Perhaps the chief purpose of a philosophy or religion is to help us understand the meaning of death and why we are alive. Without understanding where we have come from and where we are going, we cannot establish our own sense of identity to the fullest. Aging and its symptoms can, if nothing else, prompt us to seek rejuvenation. Ultimately, that rejuvenation can be found not in forestalling symptoms but in embracing a larger understanding of our own lives, which Buddhism elucidates. This principle applies in facing not only the aging process but also the third of the three sufferings—illness—which we will examine at length in the next chapter.

CHAPTER THREE:

Illness and the Medicine of Buddhism

S HAKYAMUNI is referred to in the sutras as the Great Healer because his teachings helped people overcome the sufferings of birth, aging, sickness and death. Through contemplation, Shakyamuni concluded that the best medicine is the fundamental force inherent in everyone's life, which enables us to draw forth the wisdom and energy necessary to cure our own physical and mental ills. Buddhist medicine's chief aim is to help individuals develop their natural self-healing powers by cultivating life force through Buddhist practice. While it can be viewed as medicine for the ailing human spirit, Buddhism combines harmoniously with modern Western medicine; after all, both disciplines are concerned with the alleviation of human suffering.

A Buddhist View of Health

A proverb has it that health is better than wealth. Nichiren expanded on this, writing: "More valuable than treasures in a storehouse are the treasures of the body, and the treasures of the heart are the most valuable of all."[1] It is usually only when we lose our health that we really begin to appreciate it. Even if we enjoy excellent health, though, from time to time we may experience some physical disorder. Sickness, like aging, is integral to human life. Both health and sickness coexist in our bodies. According to Western medicine, for example, our bodies both produce and eliminate cancer cells, provided that our immune system is functioning effectively.

The ancient Indian text *Caraka Samhita* proclaims freedom from sickness as an essential element of human happiness and the basis of good works, success, sexual desire and liberation from the bonds of illusion and suffering. "Freedom from sickness" here means more than the absence of illness. Good health is judged not only on physiological diagnoses but also on a holistic view of life that includes spiritual elements. As in the constitution of the World Health Organization, "Health is a state of complete physical, mental, and social well-being and not merely the absence of disease or infirmity."

Josei Toda,[2] my mentor, used to say: "A person is healthy as long as he or she can eat and sleep enough." He meant that as long as we are eating and sleeping sufficiently, we should not worry unduly about our health and instead concentrate on other matters. Toda's statement may sound simplistic, but it has definite relevance today when many people are highly sensitive about—or even morbidly afraid of—illness.

From the Mahayana Buddhist viewpoint, promoting good health is identified with the state of Bodhisattva, a condition of compassion in which we carry out selfless, altruistic actions for the benefit of humanity.

A story from the Vimalakirti Sutra (see sidebar) illustrates this. Though actually in good health, Vimalakirti, one of the Buddha's disciples, pretends to be ill out of empathy with sick and suffering beings. The message is that the bodhisattva's illness stems from his deep sense of responsibility for the sufferings of all other beings. This expresses the idea of Buddhist compassion. Buddhism teaches that good health and sickness are one and inseparable, a unifying vision illustrating the links that tie each individual to the suffering of others.

VIMALAKIRTI: THE IDEAL BODHISATTVA

Vimalakirti, who lived during Shakyamuni's time, was a wealthy lay believer. He had mastered the profound doctrines of Mahayana Buddhism and had skillfully instructed others in its ways. At one point, he became ill. Shakyamuni sent Bodhisattva Manjushri to inquire about Vimalakirti's health.

Manjushri asked: "Man of Great Virtue, what is the cause of your illness? Is it long since your illness emerged? How are you going to cure it?"

To this, Vimalakirti answered: "Because all beings are ill, I am ill. If the illnesses of all beings are eradicated, my illness will also be eradicated. The bodhisattva enters the path of birth and death for the sake of all other beings. On the path of birth and death there naturally is illness. If the beings are free from illness, the bodhisattva will also be free from illness. It is like the relationship between parents and their only child. If the child is ill, the parents will also become ill, and if the child recovers, the parents will also recover. The bodhisattva is exactly like this. When the beings are ill, the bodhisattva is ill, and when the beings recover from illness, the bodhisattva recovers as well."

Manjushri asked further: "From where does your illness originate?"

To this, Vimalakirti answered: "The sickness of the Bodhisattva arises from his great compassion."

The sutra that contains this story thus sets forth the ideal of the Mahayana bodhisattva, which is to draw no distinction between self and others.

One of Nichiren's samurai followers, Shijo Kingo, was a physician who treated Nichiren for a severe illness. Later, Nichiren wrote gratefully, "I believe that I survived this time only because Shakyamuni Buddha entered your body to help me."[3] From this comment, it seems Shijo Kingo treated his Buddhist master with great compassion.

According to Buddhism, health is not a condition in which we merely escape negative influences. It is a highly positive, active state in which we hold ourselves responsible for such influences, in which we face and try to solve various problems —not just our own but others' problems, too. The word *disease* implies a lack of ease, which conversely implies that health is a state of comfort. In the Buddhist sense, however, being "at ease" does not mean freedom from difficulties; it means having the strength to meet and overcome any problem.

Over the years, Nichiren suffered many persecutions. The last part of his life he lived on Mount Minobu, where harsh winters caused him great hardship. In a letter from there, he wrote: "For the past eight years I have become weaker year by year because of sickness and old age." Yet it was at Minobu that he fulfilled the purpose of his entire life's work: inscribing the Mystic Law in the form of a mandala called the Gohonzon, about which we'll discuss more later in the book.

Dengyo, a great Buddhist teacher of late-eighth- and early-ninth-century Japan, once wrote: "Shakyamuni taught that the shallow is easy to embrace, but the profound is difficult. To discard the shallow and seek the profound is the way of a person of courage."[4] "A person of courage" here essentially denotes the Buddha, who seeks the profound truth. "The shallow" refers to all Buddhist teachings other than the Lotus Sutra, while "the profound" means the Lotus Sutra itself—or, ultimately, the Mystic Law, which is the essence of that sutra. We can interpret this more broadly to mean that, just as the Buddha did, we should seek the profoundest way of living to achieve something equally profound in our own lives. By doing so, we shall have the strength to overcome all difficulties—a robust and healthy state of life.

Western scientists have shared a similar vision of the nature of health. René Dubos wrote in his *Mirage of Health*: "While it may be comforting to imagine a life free of stresses and strains in a carefree world, this will remain an idle dream.... Man has elected to fight, not necessarily for himself but for a process of emotional, intellectual and ethical growth that goes on forever. To grow in the midst of dangers is the fate of the human race, because it is the law of the spirit."

And the Austrian-Canadian biologist Ludwig von Bertalanffy stated in his *General System Theory*: "Life is not a comfortable settling down in preordained grooves of being; at its best, it is *élan vital*, inexorably driven towards a higher form of existence. Admittedly, this is metaphysics and poetic simile; but so, after all, is any image we try to form of the driving forces in the universe."

Regarding the purpose of disease in the drive toward perfection, the Swiss philosopher Carl Hilty said: "Just as the flooding of a river digs up the soil and nourishes the fields, illnesses serve to nourish our own hearts. A person who understands his illness correctly and perseveres through it will achieve a greater depth, strength and greatness in life."

Buddhism views illness as an opportunity to attain a higher, nobler state of life. It teaches that, instead of agonizing over a serious disease, or despairing of ever overcoming it, we should use illness as a means to build a strong, compassionate self, which in turn will make it possible for us to be truly victorious. This is what Nichiren meant when he stated, "Illness gives rise to the resolve to attain the way."[5]

Early Medicine

Health and disease have always been primary concerns of humanity. Sudden fevers, diarrhea, coughing, internal bleeding and
many other symptoms of disease that we understand better today
must have terrified our ancestors, especially as the causes for them
may have been unclear. As millennia rolled by, however, people
saw how maladies progressed and how the victims reacted. Gradually, they learned a great deal about what to do at the onset of
an illness and how to care for the ailing. This approach to medicine was based on reason, scientific in that it sought to identify
the latent healing properties of substances found in peoples' environments. Archaeological studies have shown that people often
used vegetables and herbs, animal substances and even minerals
in the remedies they concocted. Such remedies were useful for
many milder diseases, but it seems our ancestors regarded the
more serious diseases, against which their concoctions were powerless, as having a supernatural origin and requiring treatment by
magic or religious ritual. Religion therefore played an important
role in early medicine, with the duties of priest and physician
often being assumed by the same person: the shaman.

In ancient Mesopotamia, Egypt, India and China, medicine
was remarkably similar, all the different systems displaying the
characteristics just described. In ancient Greece, too, medicine
arose from a confluence of empirical and mystical traditions.
Ancient Greek civilization was strongly influenced by earlier
civilizations in Babylonia and Egypt and, to a lesser extent, in
India and China.

According to the Greeks, supernatural cures were attributed
to Asclepius, the god of medicine. His origin was traced to a
real-life Asclepius who lived around 1200 B.C.E, and who was
honored for his medical skills. Temples dedicated to Asclepius

were constructed throughout ancient Greece, and healing rituals known as "incubation," or "temple sleep," were conducted there. The sick prayed at a temple for a cure and to receive oracles from Asclepius as they slept. The temple priests, interpreting the oracles that patients received in their dreams, prescribed precise methods of treatment — usually a matter of diet, bathing and exercise. If patients recovered, they would offer a tribute to the god along with a gift symbolizing the body part that had been cured. Many of these artifacts survive at the ancient temple sites, providing a rough picture of diseases common in ancient Greece and of the treatments prescribed.

The cult of Asclepius persisted well into the Christian era. But the status of priest-physicians, or shamans, was increasingly threatened with the rise of the Greek philosophers, starting with the scientist and mystic Pythagoras (who lived around 580–500 B.C.E). Pythagoras and many Greek philosophers who followed him took a great interest in medicine. Thanks to their influence, the discipline passed from the priest-physicians to whomever actively sought the organic causes of illness, rejecting the supernatural in favor of the physical.

Hippocrates, often called the "Father of Medicine," lived about a century after Pythagoras, in a time of increasing interest in logic and reason. While teaching and practicing medicine in Athens and elsewhere in Greece, Hippocrates focused on clinical observation and rational study of the body and its various functions. An excellent physician known for his superb character, he and his followers left the ancient world the *Hippocratic Collection,* a compilation of writings representing an attitude toward life, disease and the sick person that is widely appreciated today.

Hippocrates agreed with his contemporaries that the human body — like the rest of the cosmos — was composed of the four elements, earth, water, fire and air, and that bodily dysfunctions occurred as a result of an imbalance among the four "cardinal humors"—blood, phlegm, choler (or yellow bile) and melancholy (or black bile). To simplify somewhat, Hippocrates believed that a human being is healthy when all four humors are in harmony. By contrast, when the humors fall into disharmony, the person becomes ill. Another asset of Hippocrates' ideas was his keen awareness of the body's own healing power. His attitude toward medicine is summarized in the Hippocratic oath—generally taken by students receiving a medical degree—which sets forth an ethical code for the medical profession.

Treatment of Illness in Buddhist History

As the prince of a small Indian kingdom, Shakyamuni was said to have studied medicine and thus to have acquired knowledge of the medical techniques of his day. Shakyamuni's teachings about illness are, therefore, representative of the standard of medical knowledge in ancient India. They are, moreover, based on his awareness of the true nature of life. In Indian languages, medical study was called Ayurveda, the study of longevity, and the focus of Ayurveda was to strengthen vitality, extend longevity, and increase virtue and good fortune.

There are actual cases of medical treatment described in the Buddhist sutras. Once, while the Buddha was staying in Shravasti, a monk was collecting firewood in preparation for a hot bath. As he rummaged near a dead tree, a venomous snake bit his finger. The monk, afraid that the poison would spread, promptly lopped off the finger, a troubling course of action as the Buddhist precepts prohibited mutilation of one's body. Hearing of this incident, the Buddha suggested that, should the same thing happen again, a tourniquet be applied and only the injured part of the finger be excised. This episode illustrates that the Buddha's compassion superseded his precepts.

In a different sutra, the Buddha proposed that by developing compassion snakebites could be prevented. He taught that profound mercy for all living things — even lowly life forms such as snakes, spiders and centipedes — and an indefatigable life force are important elements in preventing adversities like venomous snakebites. This focus on attitude is characteristically Buddhist; nevertheless, as the tale of the monk in Shravasti shows, Buddhism allows for commonsense solutions.

Another common affliction was an infection or abscess known as a felon, which appeared at the end of a finger or toe. Felons caused acute pain. When not properly cared for, they could spread even deeper, resulting in damage to tendons, bones and joints. Ajatashatru, a king of Magadha in Shakyamuni's time, once suffered from a deep tissue inflammation. Regarding this, his mother told him:

> When you were small, you once had a felon on your finger. It was so painful that you could sleep neither day nor night. Your father took you into his lap and placed your ailing finger in his mouth. Thus comforted by your father, you were able to sleep, and the warmth of his mouth matured the felon, finally rupturing the abscess. The Great King wondered if he should draw his mouth away from the finger to spit out the pus. But thinking that this would again cause you great pain, he instead swallowed the pus. This is what your father did for you.

Ajatashatru's father, Bimbisara, essentially used his mouth as a hot compress. Covering the finger with saliva after the rupture was especially useful, because of saliva's sterilizing effect. But far more important than physiological considerations, this episode emphasizes compassion—which, Buddhism teaches, should underlie all medical treatment.

Shakyamuni, as a matter of principle, forbade all use of the surgeon's knife, especially in the case of hemorrhoids and other ailments in the anal region. Because of the difficulty of maintaining proper hygiene, Shakyamuni's position seems entirely reasonable. He instead employed dietary and ointment therapy for afflictions in this area. But this precept was not absolute. If it was necessary that an incision be made, Shakyamuni would, for example, permit a suppurating abscess to be pricked using a lotus flower stem in order to let the pus drain out. It was only as a last resort that he would permit the use of the knife.

Then there is Jivaka, a disciple of Shakyamuni described in the sutras as the "medicine king." The accounts of his origin differ, but he is generally believed to be the son of a courtesan and an aristocrat—supposedly King Bimbisara—and that his parents abandoned him in infancy. As an adult, he studied medicine under a master physician. He could cure migraines, treat diarrhea, heal injuries of the toes and fingers, cure blindness, heal boils, operate on anal fistulas, and do other medical work.

A wealthy man in Rajagriha suffered from terrible headaches. He tried one physician after another, but none could help him, and their prognoses for his survival were not optimistic. One predicted that he had only seven years left to live, another said five years, another seven months, and yet another only a month to just a few days. In desperation, the man turned to Jivaka to cure his ailment. Jivaka must have realized the treatment would not be easy, because at first he refused. Partly because of a petition from the king, however, Jivaka eventually agreed to investigate the possibility of treating the man. He questioned the man about his condition, examined him, and concluded that the treatment had a good chance of success.

Jivaka gave the man some extremely salty food to make him very thirsty. Next, he had him drink some liquor to make him sleepy and anesthetize him. He tied the man to a bed and called in his next of kin. With a knife, Jivaka cut a hole in the man's skull and showed it to the relatives, saying: "Worms fill the entire cavity. This causes the disease. If things are left the way they are, the worms will devour the brain entirely and bring about his death within seven days." Jivaka then cut out the affected part and cleaned the region, put ghee mixed with honey into the man's head, fixed the hole in the skull, replaced the skin, stitched up the cut, and finished off the operation by applying salve to the lacerated area. The man's illness was immediately cured, and in due course the skin and hair on his head grew back so well that it was impossible to tell where the operation had been performed.

The description we have does not tell us how Jivaka cut through the skull; in view of what we know about the development of surgical instruments, however, we can assume an appropriate tool was available. The very fact that the operation was successful tells us a lot about Jivaka's skill and the high standard of Indian surgery in those days. It was only from the middle of the nineteenth century, with the advent of anesthesia and more-effective sterilization techniques, that Western surgeons began to undertake brain surgery, and even then they had many difficulties; in fact, it is only in the last several decades that we could regard brain surgery as fairly safe.

An Emphasis on Practicality

Since the earliest times, Buddhism has been noted for monastic precepts that regulated daily activities. There were precepts specifically for maintaining sanitary conditions. For example, dirt-stained robes were considered a violation of the Law, and various ways were stipulated by which robes could be washed and kept clean—according to some sutras hot water, ashes, bean powder, earth and cow dung could be used as a detergent. Bathing is frequently mentioned in the sutras, and in several forms: cold water, hot water, sauna and hot spring baths. The hot water and hot spring baths were used mostly to treat illness. Incidental details—such as when to bathe, how to wash the body, what to use as soap—were precisely stipulated in the form of precepts.

Physical exercise was valued as an aid to digestion, concentration and clear thinking. Rinsing one's nose, washing one's eyes and brushing one's teeth were regarded as essential daily health care. Condensed milk, oils and fats were used for cleansing. These practices were regarded as important also in the treatment of headaches, eye diseases and other ailments. Nagarjuna, a Mahayana scholar, is said to have lived an extremely long life, partly due to rinsing his nose every day. And Shakyamuni stressed the importance of sufficient sleep and eating in moderation.

In sum, then, we should note the practicality of Buddhist medicine, its concern with maintaining good health and healing the body. Shakyamuni never resorted to faith healing or instructing the sick to perform magic rituals. Instead, he laid out scientific, rational ways of dealing with people's injuries and diseases. This exemplifies the fundamental Buddhist attitude toward life. For those who suffered from ailments medicine could not cure, Shakyamuni told them not to despair but to cultivate their healing power by bringing forth the Buddhahood inherent in their lives.

Buddhist medicine originated from Buddhism, prospered with the rise of Buddhism and, as Buddhism declined in India, it likewise fell into disrepute. As the vigorous Buddhist drive to save the people disappeared, so did the religion's power to impact people's lives. Buddhists instead became focused on formality and doctrinal studies. The great role Buddhist medicine played in people's daily lives, now glimpsed only dimly in the sutras, is today overshadowed by the glories of modern Western allopathic medicine.

Recently, however, aspects of Chinese medicine, notably acupuncture and moxa cautery, have attracted the attention of the West, bringing to light people's misgivings about the limits and deficiencies of Western medicine. In the same way, greater understanding of Buddhist medicine can broaden the horizons of Western physicians—not through advances in technology but through a new philosophy or attitude toward health and life that can serve as the backbone of a truly modern medicine. Fusion of the wisdom of East and West would contribute greatly to the prosperity and happiness of every human being on this planet.

The Five Components of Life

Buddhism views human beings as the temporary union of five components—form, perception, conception, volition and consciousness. Buddhism holds that these five aspects, also known as the five aggregates (or *skandhas* in Sanskrit), unite temporarily to form an individual living being. All life carries on its activities through the interaction of these five components. Their workings are affected by the karma we have formed in previous lifetimes, and it is through their workings that we continuously create new karma.

Form represents the physical aspect of life and includes the eyes, ears, nose, tongue and body with which one perceives the external world. The other four components represent the mental or spiritual aspect. *Perception* is the function of receiving external information through the six sense organs—the five senses plus the mind, which integrates the impressions of the five senses. *Conception* is the function of creating mental images and concepts out of what has been perceived. *Volition* is the will that acts on conception and motivates action. *Consciousness* is the function of discernment that integrates the components of perception, conception and volition.

Form, life's physical aspect, is said to be composed of the four elements: earth, water, fire and wind. Sometimes space (or emptiness) is added to the list of elements, bringing them up to five. The four elements can also be understood in terms of their natures or functions. Each corresponds to a quality of matter: earth to hardness, water to wetness, fire to heat or warmth, and wind to movement or fluidity. Nichiren wrote: "The function of fire is to burn and give light. The function of water is to wash away filth. The winds blow away dust and breathe life into plants, animals, and human beings. The earth produces the grasses and trees, and heaven provides nourishing moisture."[6] The element earth is represented in the external world by mountains, rocks, sand, pebbles and such; in the internal world of the body earth is represented by the skin, hair, nails, teeth and bones. The element water manifests itself in the world as rivers and seas, while in terms of the body it appears as blood and other bodily fluids. Fire is found in our planet's crust in the form of volcanoes and igneous intrusions, but it is felt, too, as body temperature and in the digestion process. Wind is apparent externally in the fluidity of the air and internally in the body's respiration and metabolism.

The four elements represent four intrinsic forces inherent in the universe. The confluence of their fundamental energies was thought, in traditional Buddhism, to underlie all material changes in the world.

THE FIVE COMPONENTS

A living being is formed when the five components temporarily unite. They are:

PHYSICAL ASPECT OF LIFE

+ *Form* includes the eyes, ears, nose, tongue and body with which one perceives the external world.

SPIRITUAL ASPECT OF LIFE

+ *Perception* is the function of receiving external information through the six sense organs.

+ *Conception* is the function of creating mental images and concepts out of what has been perceived.

+ *Volition* is the will that acts on conception and motivates action.

+ *Consciousness* is the function of discernment that integrates the components of perception, conception and volition.

Nichiren teaches that the five elements (the four elements and space) symbolically correspond to the five characters that make up Myoho-renge-kyo. The fact that the universe and each human being comprise these five elements suggests that the individual body and the universe share the same essence, which Nichiren identifies as the Mystic Law, or Myoho-renge-kyo.

Disease can be interpreted as a state of internal disharmony among the five elements. Therefore, Buddhism considers how the individual can keep the elements in harmonious balance. It teaches that our internal environment is ultimately inseparable from our external one, and that external disharmony can directly affect our internal condition. To be healthy, we must have the flexibility and endurance to withstand the ill effects of external influences such as stress and pathogens; we need to maintain internal stability regardless of what is happening in our environment. Calling forth one's Buddha nature is said to counteract ill effects and harmonize the constituent elements of one's life, thus providing internal stability. This Buddha nature is the self-regulating—or all-regulating—essence of life, or pure life force. When we tap into this life force—as Nichiren teaches, by chanting Nam-myoho-renge-kyo—we can "get in rhythm" with the universe and enhance our vibrancy and strength. This is the Buddhist ideal of good health.

Causes of Illness

In Buddhism, illnesses are classified in many ways. Some sutras categorize them according to the element whose imbalance is thought to be the cause. Others, according to the part of the body affected. And yet other sutras classify illnesses according to the time they were caused—that is, they differentiate between diseases caused in this lifetime and those whose causes can be found in previous lifetimes. For example, according to Nagarjuna's *Treatise on the Great Perfection of Wisdom*, diseases are divided into karmic diseases and present diseases, the latter category being subdivided into diseases of the body and diseases of the mind. Diseases of the body are yet further subdivided into internal diseases (arising from internal causes) and external diseases (whose causes are external to the body).

T'ien-t'ai, the great sixth-century Chinese Buddhist teacher, suggests six causes of illness that cover problems arising from dietary habits, viral infections (such as polio), mental disorders and genetic heritage.

Nichiren based his own teachings concerning illness upon

CAUSES OF ILLNESS

Nichiren based his teachings on illness on T'ien-t'ai's classifications:

DISEASES OF THE BODY

✦ disharmony of the four elements

✦ improper eating or drinking

✦ poor posture or irregular meditation

✦ attack of demons

DISEASES OF THE MIND

✦ the work of devils

KARMIC DISEASES

✦ the effects of karma

this systematic presentation of the Buddhist view of disease and its causes. In a writing called "Curing Karmic Disease," he quoted from T'ien-t'ai's *Great Concentration and Insight*: "There are six causes of illness: (1) disharmony of the four elements; (2) improper eating or drinking; (3) poor posture; (4) attack of demons; (5) the work of devils; and (6) the effects of karma."

In this classification, the first four causes correspond to illnesses of the body, the fifth to illnesses of the mind, and the sixth to karmic illness.

The classification of diseases in modern medicine is, of course, far more systematic and thorough than what is presented in the Buddhist scriptures and treatises. The Buddhist approach to medicine can be considered scientific, however, in that it takes into account cause-and-effect relationships. And, while modern medicine tends to view the ailing part of the body in isolation from the rest, treating it alone as if repairing a malfunctioning machine part, Buddhist medicine views disease as a reflection of the total body system, or life itself, and seeks to cure it not only through medical treatment but also through adjustments in the person's lifestyle and outlook.

Illnesses of the Body

The first cause, among the six causes of illness described above, are sicknesses resulting from disharmony among the four elements—earth, water, fire and wind—that make up the human body and that correspond to the physical states: solid, liquid, thermal and gaseous.

Disharmony of the four elements refers both to disharmony within the body and to disharmony between the body and its natural environment. This latter can result from an inability to adapt to changes in the external environment—weather, for example. Any disruption of this natural harmony can cause physical disease.

Improper eating or drinking and poor posture (also described as irregular meditation)—the second and third causes of illness—might be viewed as examples of an unbalanced way of life. These would include such things as illnesses arising from poor diet and immoderate consumption of food or drink, or disturbances in the rhythm of our lives—such as insufficient sleep and exercise—which make us susceptible to getting sick.

The fourth cause of illness T'ien-t'ai mentions is quite interesting. "Attack of demons" refers to attacks from outside the body from any of the many external forces or influences that can cause physical suffering or even death. For example, invasive pathogenic bacteria or viruses, or even the modern notion of stress, both now widely known to cause many illness would be considered demons in this sense.

Illnesses of the Mind

The fifth cause of disease is the working of "devils" from within that manifest in the form of mental illness.

The concept of devils and their role in illness bears some exploration. Devil (or *mara* in Sanskrit) is often translated as "the destroyer" or "robber of life." Devils in Buddhist mythology are personifications of negative internal functions. They represent selfish attachments and bad influences that hinder people's pursuit of truth and that work to prevent them from cultivating a strong, positive life force. Devilish functions are aspects of our own lives that damage our health and hamper the practice of Buddhist teachings.

Devils represent the fundamental tendency of an individual's life toward disharmony of body and mind. Unlike the other four causes of illness, this affects the realm of the mind. Its source is located not in external influences but within the individual, so that the person's life is robbed of its brilliance. The result is the emergence of life's fundamental darkness or delusion.

From darkness and delusion arise the three poisons—greed, anger and foolishness. These poisons are understood as the source of all destructive, selfish desires or attachments, and are essentially devilish.

Greed sends all five sense organs off in a perpetual, insatiable, search for gratification—wealth, love, food, fame, idleness and so on— draining us of innate life force. When our lives are dominated by greed, all our energy is directed toward the object of our desire, weakening us as if the blood were draining from our bodies.

Anger indicates malice born of hatred, which prevents one's heart from turning to goodness and disturbs the harmonious relationship between self and others. This disturbance can lead to conflict of colossal proportions, engendering strife and war that may eventually destroy our lives.

Foolishness means ignorance of one's own Buddha nature and is characterized by blindness to the law of cause and effect, as well as shortsighted attachment to immediate gain. Foolishness prevents people from seeing the damage an unwise way of living has caused to their bodies and minds.

These three poisons are among what Buddhism terms the basic illusions or "earthly desires." Each is accompanied by

THE THREE POISONS

The source of all illusions and earthly desires, called poisons because they pollute people's lives and work to prevent them from turning their hearts and minds to good.

GREED

Sends all five sense organs off in a perpetual, but insatiable, search for gratification — wealth, love, food, fame, idleness, and so on — draining us of innate life force.

ANGER

Indicates malice born of hatred disturbing the harmonious relationship between self and others.

FOOLISHNESS

Ignorance of one's own Buddha nature and characterized by blindness to the law of cause and effect, as well as shortsighted attachment to immediate gain.

specific traits. Greed, for example, is associated with miserliness, self-indulgence, guilt, deceit and adulation. Anger brings about resentment, hatred, irritation, jealousy and the urge to harm other living beings. Twenty such specific traits are identified in Buddhism, and they in turn give rise to an even greater variety of destructive qualities that can disrupt the harmony of life to where we become extremely ill in body or mind—or both. The varied ways in which mental illnesses arise and the complexity of the workings of all these destructive qualities give rise to what are said to be 84,000 types of mental illness as opposed to a mere 404 types of physiological illness.

Another way of looking at earthly desires is in terms of three categories of illusions: illusions of thought and desire, illusions as uncountable as particles of dust and sand, and illusions about the true nature of existence.

Illusions of thought are primarily mental and acquired, while the *illusions of desire* are chiefly emotional and inherent. Illusions of thought refer to false perceptions of the truth. These can take several forms, including such erroneous notions as regarding our present existence as absolute, even though our bodies are formed from a temporary union of the five components; believing that we own forever what does not in fact belong to us; believing either that life ends at the moment of death or that it persists beyond death in some eternally unchanging form; not recognizing the law of cause and effect; and adhering to misconceptions with such closed-mindedness that we regard inferior things as superior. Illusions of desire can be summarized much more briefly: they include base emotions such as greed, anger, foolishness and arrogance arising in connection with specific objects or events.

The *illusions as uncountable as particles of dust and sand* are those that arise as we practice Buddhism with the intention to help others. While recognizing the truth of Buddhist principles, we may at times feel they aren't applicable to certain people's situations. Or we may lack confidence in sharing what we have learned. Yet, conquering these difficulties is the bodhisattva way. When we can fully express our wisdom in dealing directly with every aspect of our lives, including sharing the teachings, we are expressing our Buddhahood.

Illusions about the true nature of existence prevent bodhisattvas from awakening to their true nature. These illusions reside in the deepest reaches of the unconscious, and they have the devastating potential to cast our lives into total darkness, depriving us of the illumination of compassion and wisdom and leading to self-destruction. Illusions about the true nature of existence generate the impulse to kill and destroy, or as the still more primitive urge to sacrifice others and even delight in doing so. Buddhism teaches that living on the basis of such impulses is in itself a mental illness.

Just as our physical condition affects our mental state, our bodily health is greatly affected by the beliefs (or delusions) we hold and our attitude toward life—factors that originate in the mind. We can therefore conclude that while the mind is a supremely powerful factor in our health condition, at the same time it is especially subtle and susceptible to external influences. Replacing the illusions arising from the three poisons with wisdom, courage and confidence generated by Buddhist practice becomes an important aspect of strengthening and sustaining our spiritual health—the foundation of physical and mental well-being.

Karmic Disease

The first five causes of illness originate in this present lifetime. The sixth cause, the effects of karma, is very different because its origins lie in our previous existences. Karmic diseases can manifest as either mental or physical illness and are very difficult, if not impossible, to cure through traditional methods.

The concept of karma was not developed so that we would resign ourselves to hopeless suffering. By correctly understanding the notion of karma, we automatically come to recognize that we are responsible for whatever problems we face in life and that we ourselves must strive to overcome those problems. This recognition enables us to establish true independence. In the case of karmic diseases, beyond merely searching for better medicine or changing our outlook, we must act to eradicate the negative karma at the root of the illness, and by so doing cause the illness to disappear.

Descriptions of the various karmic diseases have changed over time and should continue to do so. For example, the sutras considered leprosy a karmic disease because in Shakyamuni's time it was incurable, and victims suffered not only physical torment—likely disfigurement and death—but also considerable mental anguish through the loathing and ostracism of their fellow citizens. Today, however, leprosy can be controlled, and those who have it can lead relatively normal lives. Many other diseases have been virtually eradicated thanks to modern medicine—tuberculosis is another example. Still, there are many incurable diseases, and newer ones, such as AIDS, appear continually. Some are born out of the development of society, and some even arise from medical treatment itself.

Medical science will probably never eliminate all diseases. More likely, some will always remain a mystery; and humankind may always have to cope with incurable diseases and face the fear of death. From a secular perspective, anyway, karmic disease is an unavoidable enigma. Buddhist practice, which seeks to activate our inner life force at the most fundamental level, offers a key to overcoming all six types of illness, especially karmic illness, because it effects change in one's karma itself.

Often, people living in the same time period, in the same community, or belonging to the same class will experience a common predicament. When this occurs, we can say they share a "collective" karma. If a group or nation shares common but mistaken beliefs, they will share a common fate. Epidemics, for example, arise from commonly held misunderstandings about diet, sanitation and such. While recognizing the collective nature of such dilemmas, Buddhism asserts that the remedy for all problems begins with the individual's change in perspective and the actions he or she takes based on that inner reformation. As each of us awakens to our limitless power within, we can exert an ever-greater influence on our environment and bring about a change in the minds of our fellow human beings that can effect a change in the destiny of all humankind.

Three Functions of the Mystic Law

According to the Lotus Sutra, even a Buddha who embodies the ideal state of life will never be completely free of ailments. What ultimately matters is our ability to mobilize the innate healing power of our lives.

The cultivation of this healing power depends on our individual will. The role of will in curing a person's illness is becoming ever more apparent. For example, if we are shocked and weakened when we discover we have a serious disease, we are much more likely to succumb to it than if we refuse to accept the news as a death sentence and elect to fight the disease. Our willpower affects our body's ability to produce natural "medicines"—hormones, enzymes and antibodies—which it marshals to combat negative influences and preserve life.

Willpower thus has a major part to play in helping us take full advantage of our native healing abilities. Willpower in this sense refers to how deeply we can grasp, how strongly we can tap into, the true aspect of our lives, which, according to Buddhism, comprises infinite potential and cosmic scale. This type of willpower derives from absolute confidence in the vastness of our existence, and a strong sense of purpose and responsibility to this world.

The strength of Buddhist medicine lies in the development of the Buddha nature from within, which provides the key to activating the unlimited potentials and energies inherent in the individual human life.

Myo, a syllable of *myoho* (as in Nam-myoho-renge-kyo) means "mystic" or "beyond comprehension," and it describes a continually creative force that pulses in every healthy entity, sustaining its activity. This force has three general characteristics: renewal, perfection and openness.

As Nichiren implied by writing "*Myo* means to revive, that is, to return to life,"[7] the Mystic Law—Nam-myoho-renge-kyo —enables us to unleash new life force from within. In a broader sense, this indicates that we have the power to transform ourselves from sickly persons into healthy and happy ones.

Nichiren also wrote: "*Myo* means to be fully endowed, which in turn has the meaning of 'perfect and full.'... To illustrate, one drop of the great ocean contains within it the waters of all the various rivers that flow into the ocean, and a single wish-granting jewel, though no bigger than a mustard seed, is capable of showering down the treasures that one could wish for with all the wish-granting jewels."[8] Each of our individual lives is fully endowed with all of the potential that exists in the cosmos. When the Mystic Law is brought into play, it orchestrates our spiritual and physical functions in superb harmony, vitalizing our vast innate potential. As a result, the greatest healing influence — our own unhampered life force — rises to the occasion and enables us to overcome even the most virulent disease.

Nichiren explained the third characteristic of *myo*:

> The Lotus Sutra says, "This sutra opens the gate of expedient means and shows the form of true reality." The Great Teacher Chang-an states, "*Myo* means to reveal the depths of the secret storehouse." The Great Teacher Miao-lo says of this, "To reveal means to open." Hence the character *myo* means to open.[9]

In the context of health, this passage explains that the Mystic Law enables us to reveal "the depths of the secret storehouse," which is the Buddha nature, and "open" our existence to the environment. In other words, we can establish a foundation from which we can always actively and positively engage with our environment, transmuting all of its influences into beneficial ones.

To sum up, then, these three characteristics of the Mystic Law are: to activate our inherent life force; to harmonize our spiritual and physical functions; and to equip us with the resources to influence our environment for the better while responding to its myriad changes with wisdom and maintaining a balance between it and ourselves. When we base our lives on this Law — by practicing Buddhism as Nichiren teaches — we can tap the limitless power inside ourselves so that disease is no longer a matter for despair. In fact, the opposite is true: empowered by the Mystic Law we can transform disease into a source of growth, joy and true fulfillment.

THREE PROPERTIES OF 'MYO'

The character *myo*, meaning mystic or beyond comprehension, describes a continually creative force inherent in all life. It has three characteristics:

✦ Renewal, a self-motivated capacity for creativity, demonstrated in how the human body constantly responds in new ways and rallies its creative resources.

✦ Perfection, in the sense of wholeness and unity; completion. The dynamic equilibrium of the human body as a whole—its homeostasis — is perfectly balanced and an expression to the mystic force.

✦ Openness, or the individual's ability to influence his or her environment. Every living thing reacts to and is capable of provoking a reaction in its external environment.

Looking Ahead

No one can deny modern medicine's contributions to the curing of disease. It would be foolish to ignore it. Otherwise, faith descends into fanaticism.

Yet, for all its impressive technology, effective pharmaceuticals and elaborate diagnostic techniques, modern medical science is not omnipotent. Moreover, its treatments often tend toward a materialistic or mechanistic view of the human organism, neglecting to look at life as a phenomenon involving both body and mind. Whereas modern medicine largely relies on drugs and technology, Buddhist medicine concentrates on the patient's role in curing his or her own illness. We might say that medical science fights illness with scientific knowledge, while Buddhism develops human wisdom so that we may find our own rhythm and strengthen our life force. This assists the efficacy of medical treatment and also helps us conquer illness through our own natural healing powers.

We must use medical resources wisely in fighting illness. Buddhism gives us the wisdom to use medicine properly. Wisdom is the basic ingredient to health, to long life and to happiness.

In general, we can say that Buddhist medicine focuses on three aspects: 1) developing the conditions of Buddhahood, 2) achieving and maintaining harmony of the four elements within our bodies as well as with our external environment, and 3) achieving and maintaining harmony among the five components.

Buddhism regards disease as an external manifestation of internal disharmony. Further, Buddhist medicine maintains that the quality of human life or health is determined by the balance of an indescribably vast number of factors, each in a constant state of flux. Establishing equilibrium among these factors is little short of miraculous; so it is hardly surprising that the balance is disturbed periodically, resulting in illness. The strength of Buddhist medicine is that it focuses on activating the unlimited potentials and energies inherent in the individual human life to restore and sustain this robust, dynamic equilibrium.

When we access our fundamental life force, no illness can prevent us from living a fulfilling life. In the next chapter, we discuss the Buddhist view of what comes after that.

CHAPTER FOUR

Death

THE THOUGHT of death, the inescapable reminder of the finite nature of our existence, weighs heavily on the human heart. However limitless our wealth or power might seem, the reality of our eventual demise cannot be avoided. During our lives, we experience transience as the sufferings of birth (and day-to-day existence), aging, sickness and finally death. No human being is exempt from these sources of pain.

It was, in fact, human distress — in particular the problem of death — that spawned the formation of religious and philosophical systems. Shakyamuni, in his accidental encounters with life's sorrows, glimpsed a dead body and was inspired to seek truth. Plato stated that true philosophers are always engaged in the practice of dying; and Nichiren admonishes us to "first study death, then study other matters."[1]

Death Seen from a Larger Context

Modern civilization has attempted to ignore death. We have diverted our gaze from this most fundamental of concerns, attempting to drive death into the shadows. For many people, death is the mere absence of life; it is blankness; it is the void. Life is identified with all that is good: with being, rationality and light. In contrast, death is perceived as evil, as nothingness, and as the dark and irrational. The negative perception of death prevails.

We cannot, however, ignore death. Today, many issues demand a re-examination and re-evaluation of death's significance. These include questions about brain death and death with dignity, the function of hospices, alternative funerary styles and rites, and research into death and dying by writers such as Elisabeth Kübler-Ross.

We finally seem ready to recognize the fundamental error in our view of life and death. We are beginning to understand that death is more than the absence of life; that death, together with active life, is necessary for the formation of a larger, more essential whole. This greater whole reflects the deeper continuity of life and death that we experience as individuals and express as a culture. Our central challenge is to establish a culture based on understanding the relationship of life, death and eternity. Instead of disowning death, we would thereby confront and correctly position it within the larger context of life.

Buddhism speaks of an intrinsic Buddha nature existing in the depths of phenomenal reality. This nature depends upon and responds to phenomenal conditions, and it alternates between states of emergence and latency. All phenomena, including life and death, can be seen as elements of the cycle of emergence and latency, or manifestation and withdrawal.

Cycles of life and death can be likened to the alternating periods of sleep and wakefulness. Just as sleep prepares us for the next day's activity, death can be seen as a state in which we rest and replenish ourselves for new life. In this light, death should be acknowledged, along with life, as a blessing to be appreciated.

The Lotus Sutra, the core of Mahayana Buddhism, states that the purpose of existence, the eternal cycles of life and death, is to be "happy and at ease."² It further teaches that sustained faith and practice enable us to know a deep and abiding joy in death as well as in life, to be equally "happy and at ease" with both. Nichiren describes the attainment of this state as the "greatest of all joys."³

The Buddhist View of the Eternity of Life

Since, according to the Buddhist view, life is eternal, death is not so much the cessation of an existence as the beginning of a new one. In a brief essay called "Philosophy of Life," Josei Toda put forward his ideas on the eternity of life. He vividly described his incarceration as a prisoner of conscience during World War II and told of how he awakened to many of life's truths:

> While detained in a cold prison on ungrounded accusations, living a life of loneliness and isolation, I meditated day after day and month after month on the ultimate nature of life. What is life? Is life eternal? Does it exist in this world alone? Wise men and holy men throughout the ages have pondered these great riddles, each attempting to solve them in his own way.
>
> In the filth of prison, lice breed prolifically. One day, as if invited by the balmy spring sunshine, several lice strolled out lightheartedly.... I crushed one of them with my fingernail, but the others were still nonchalantly moving. Where did the life that had animated the creature go? Did it disappear forever from this world?⁴

Next, he described his first encounter with Nichiren's philosophy after having researched various spiritual teachings. Toda wrote about a great moment of insight he achieved as a result of having chanted Nam-myoho-renge-kyo two million times over the course of several months while continually contemplating the Lotus Sutra. Through this insight, he acquired a direct understanding of the truth that life is indeed eternal.

> Such writings [which assume life is eternal] are innumerable. Without this conception, there is no Buddhism. This is what life really is and the first gate for sages' enlightenment. Many intellectuals may scoff at the Buddhist idea of life, denying it as superstition, but I am afraid that, in taking this attitude, they only reveal their own thoughtless and basically unscientific approach. The law of causality is essential to science. All phenomena in the universe are governed by the law of cause and effect; therefore, to ignore this law by stating that life is no more than the result of the union of spermatozoon and ovum is superficial because it only explains appearances, failing to take into account a certain original cause. If one is prepared to conclude that life occurs fortuitously and disappears like a bubble, while assuming that every other phenomenon is ruled by cause and effect, it must be said that one's attitude is amazingly insensitive to the nature of life itself.
>
> Some people are brilliant by birth, others not. Some are beautiful, others not. Some are healthy, others not. There are many distinctions. Some are poor despite their efforts to be successful. Some suffer from earthly desires like greed or jealousy, which cannot be alleviated by means of science or social institutions. These differences must have fundamental causes; therefore, humanity's problems cannot be solved without a thorough investigation into the nature of life.[5]

Near-Death Experiences

Today, there is increasing evidence suggesting some level of existence beyond clinical death, as scientists and those who have undergone near-death experiences (and whose accounts have been recorded in innumerable books, articles and interviews) will attest.

Research into near-death experiences deals primarily with the impressions of people who have come back to life after having been pronounced clinically dead, and with documenting how people adjust to the reality of impending death.

Since 1975, when the American internist Raymond A. Moody Jr. published *Life After Life: The Investigation of a Phenomenon, Survival of Bodily Death*, many physicians, psychologists and psychiatrists have published data on the same phenomenon. Dr. Moody derived the following basic patterns from the experiences he collected. The most commonly experienced phenomena include the sensation of passing through a long tunnel just when the doctor pronounces the subject dead, followed by sudden consciousness of separation from the physical body, encounters with others, recollections of major life events and the appearance of life as light. Later research has shown that these patterns are generally shared.

As recounted in *Life After Life*, a patient interviewed in one study described his experience: "I was in an utterly black, dark void. It is very difficult to explain, but I felt as if I were moving in a vacuum, just through blackness. Yet, I was quite conscious. It was like being in a cylinder that had no air in it. It was a feeling of limbo, of being halfway here, and halfway somewhere else."[6]

This is only one among many similar accounts. Together they strongly indicate that, despite all appearances to the contrary, life, as a subjective experience, is not in fact extinguished at the moment of death.

Of course, at this point, researchers have not yet come to any definite conclusion as to the meaning of near-death experiences. Broadly speaking, there are two schools of thought. One postulates that some form of consciousness continues after death. The other holds that all near-death experiences can be explained as neurological phenomena. Scientists who adopt this latter position argue that near-death experiences do not necessarily point to the existence of an afterlife.

Certainly, discussions of the hereafter are speculative since the existence of such a realm cannot be proven empirically — it is but a theory. Conversely, there are no grounds to assert that a materialist view of life, which postulates that life ends at death, is any more scientific or less speculative than the view that life continues after death. Neither view can be fully substantiated.

This brings to mind the argument put forward by Blaise Pascal, the French thinker and mathematician who described human beings as "thinking reeds." Pascal is well known for his work in probability theory. True to his intellectual proclivities, he discussed life after death in terms of a wagering theory.

Intelligence, said Pascal, cannot provide an answer as to whether there is an afterlife. If people gamble their lives on the chance that there is life after death, then, even if they are wrong, they haven't lost anything. On the other hand, if they gamble their life on the chance that there is no afterlife, and it turns out that in fact there is, then they are powerless to alter the course they have taken. Even if, for the sake of the hereafter, they wish to have done more good things while alive, it is too late — they are left helpless and empty-handed. Pascal therefore concluded that it makes the most sense to lay one's stakes on the belief that there is life after death, in other words, to accept religion; and that this is the choice that any rational person would make.

This argument may be controversial, but Pascal's reasoning seems persuasive.

No matter how we interpret near-death experiences, the lives of people who have undergone them have been revolutionized. Some have reported that a face-to-face encounter with death caused them to reflect critically on the way they had been living and to try to live as fully as possible, so as to be prepared for death whenever it might come.

In general, people who have returned from death's doorstep tend to have a marked change in attitude. They no longer fear dying. They spend much of their remaining time in the pursuit of knowledge. And, no longer egotistically concerned with fame, power or wealth, they resolve to live altruistically and compassionately.

Stages of Preparing for Death

Awareness that life is eternal, or that one's life is interrelated with the lives of all others, or that life can be as expansive as the universe offers immense spiritual comfort and enhances the quality of our lives. In recent years, much attention has been focused on training that prepares people for the inevitability of death. Participants in workshops and seminars have engaged in various exercises; for example, role-playing in which they are told they have only six months to live. They then have to decide how they would spend those final six months. In another exercise, people rank the three most important things in life to them. These techniques suggest that thinking about death involves a refocusing on life.

Dr. Elisabeth Kübler-Ross is widely regarded as a pioneer in the clinical study of death. She contends that terminally ill patients generally pass through five stages as they approach death. Upon first hearing they are terminally ill, most patients respond with shock and a refusal to believe that the diagnosis is correct; they often change their doctors many times, hoping to be reassured that their condition is not in fact fatal. The second stage involves anger. Patients accept the fact that they will die but then become angry with the people around them and per-haps also with their god for letting their prayers for recovery go unheeded. In the third stage patients try to bargain with their god or fate in an effort to prolong their lives. This phase might be seen as a time of truce. The fourth stage is characterized by depression. As death seems imminent, patients gradually sink into a deep depression known technically as "preparatory grief."

After these four, the patient enters the fifth and final stage: acceptance. If patients lack moral support or care during the crucial period before acceptance, or if they are isolated, say, in a hospital, they will almost certainly slump into depression. On the other hand, patients who have accepted their fate will pre-pare themselves to die with peace and dignity. Patients who have strong faith—whatever the religion, including those that give no credence to the idea of an afterlife—tend to die more calmly than those who have no religious beliefs.

Many people, Kübler-Ross says, approach death feeling angry or depressed. Those who resist death to the very last moment may create more agony for themselves; and those who superficially accept the fact of their dying, merely resigning themselves to fate, will likely die far less peacefully than those who have genuinely accepted that this life will end soon. Until the last moment, they may cling to the faint hope that they might not die.

Conversely, coming face to face with death can awaken

positive feelings of compassion or benevolence. At the end of our lives, positive and negative energies gush forth from our unconscious, or what Buddhism refers to as the "*alaya*-consciousness," or storehouse of karmic effects. Often, negative emotions overwhelm positive ones; in order to control negativity, we have to transform it, we have to strengthen the positive energy.

This is where full understanding of the teachings of Buddhism can help us to prepare for death. In one of Nichiren's writings, we find the following passage:

> Nagarjuna explains the character *myo* of *myoho*, or Mystic Law, saying, "It is like a great physician who can turn poison into medicine…." Poison means the three paths of earthly desires, karma and sufferings of life. Medicine means the three virtues of the Buddha: the Dharma body, wisdom, and emancipation or freedom. To turn poison into medicine means to change the three paths into the three virtues.[7]

This passage implies that the ultimate Law of the universe can change the negative aspects of life, as represented by the three paths, into positive aspects, as characterized by the three virtues.

Transforming the Three Paths Into the Three Virtues

According to the teaching of the three paths (earthly desires, karma, suffering), the desire to reduce suffering inspires action. If that action is based on delusions about the true nature of life, then unwise actions will be taken (negative karma created), resulting in negative effects increasing rather than receding. As a result, suffering in the lower six worlds is aggravated instead of reduced as one intended. When suffering intensifies, the desire to reduce it gets even stronger. Stuck in this endless cycle, people continue to suffer despite their efforts. Many schools of Buddhism, based on understandings generally depicted as the three paths, guide practitioners toward eliminating desire as the means to break this cycle and reduce suffering.

Nichiren recognized, however, that the elimination of desire is ultimately a dead end, as some desires, in fact, create value and some sustain life. He proposed that the problem is not desire but rather delusion about the true nature of life. In Nichiren's teaching of the three virtues (truth, wisdom, emancipation), desires based on truth rather than delusion give rise to wise actions (good karma), which reduce the negative effects of our karma and free us of suffering. As we gain actual experience with this principle, faith in this truth grows even stronger. As a result, desires lead to enlightenment, not suffering.

Thus, for Nichiren Buddhism practitioners, desires represent the motivating force of life. The impetus for breaking from the three paths and living life with the three virtues is found in the elimination of delusion, not the elimination of desire. Even the sufferings normally associated with the death process can be transformed.

The Process of Dying

When we pass through the portal of death—the gateway between this life and the next—both our physical condition and our psychological state are profoundly affected. The manner in which we partake of this passage also has a crucial impact on the conditions into which our lives are reborn.

As noted in the chapter on birth, Buddhism recognizes four stages of existence to which all forms of life are subject: existence during birth; existence during life; existence during death; and existence between death and rebirth, or the intermediate existence. Existence during death is therefore considered as quite distinct from existence during life, implying that the phase of death is completely different from that of living.

As we pass through death to the intermediate existence, our being is transformed. Gradually, our sense organs fail; we can

THREE PATHS INTO THE THREE VIRTUES

The three paths are:

+ Earthly desires

+ Karma

+ Suffering

They are called paths because one leads to the other. Earthly desires give rise to actions that create evil karma, which in turn manifests itself as suffering, which aggravates earthly desires and so on in an endless cycle.

Nichiren taught that faith in the Lotus Sutra and the chanting of Nam-myoho-renge-kyo can transform the three paths into the three virtues:

+ Dharma body—the truth the Buddha realized

+ Wisdom—the wisdom to realize the truth

+ Emancipation—freedom from the sufferings of birth and death

Thus the three virtues are inseparable from the three paths. Therefore, Nichiren taught, there is no need to eliminate the three paths; all one has to do is to manifest their true nature, which is ultimately the three virtues.

no longer see, hear or feel. The functions of consciousness that integrate our sensory perceptions and maintain our sense of individual ego also fade; our name, address and bank account, among other things, become irrelevant. The effects of our karma, which are the basis of the ego, continue to influence us even after our death as well as determine what the next life-time will be like.

All our actions in this lifetime are condensed at the moment of death into something like a karmic seed with the potential to sprout and blossom in our future existences. In a rapid recollection at the moment of our death—what some who have had near-death experiences have referred to as life flashing in front of their eyes—we are compelled to reflect upon our past. We will review our behavior stemming from greed and anger, which are rooted in the fundamental darkness inherent in humanity; indignation, grudges, distress, jealousy and personal antipathy, for example, etch negative karma into our lives.

In the general turmoil of dying, we may become frightened and confused and struggle frantically. We may feel many emotions—contentment, dissatisfaction, joy, sadness and regret. How we live prepares us for this moment, and Buddhist practice teaches us how and sustains our ability to live well.

From a Buddhist perspective, our ability to pass successfully through the dying process depends upon our steady efforts during life to accumulate good causes and effects and to strengthen the foundation of goodness in the depths of our lives. We can enter the intermediate existence peacefully and joyfully if, at the time of death, we are awakened to our fundamental Buddha nature. Nichiren encouraged this attitude: "Be resolved to summon forth the great power of faith, and chant Nam-myoho-renge-kyo with the prayer that your faith will be steadfast and correct at the moment of death."[8]

Faith at the Time of Death

Clinical death is thought to occur at the moment when death becomes irrevocable, a moment signaled by physiological symptoms such as the death of the brain stem and the cessation of breathing and the heartbeat. At this moment, the individual is believed to be experiencing death. Mental and physical energies all disintegrate, and the deceased's life and karmic energy continue on into a state of non-substantiality.

Nichiren Buddhism teaches the way to empower the individual in this state. If relatives and friends chant Nam-myoho-renge-kyo through the final moments leading to clinical death, the dying person is helped to peacefully undergo the process of death. Hearing the chant, mingling with its vibration or energy, the deceased passes into the intermediate existence and toward the eternal life-flow that is the universe.

Since our karma at the time of death is important, faith in the Mystic Law can fundamentally transform suffering into an elevated state of life. Thus Nichiren recommends that Buddhists develop the habit of chanting Nam-myoho-renge-kyo with the deep conviction that one's life is, in essence, identical with the life of Buddhahood. He wrote: "If one attains full awakening to the truth that the mind of common mortals and the mind of the Buddha are one, neither will evil karma obstruct his dying in peace nor will distracting thoughts bind him to the cycle of birth and death."⁹

Nichiren taught that the effects accumulated through chanting Nam-myoho-renge-kyo far transcend the dimension of ordinary good or evil karma. Thus, irrespective of sufferings or calamities we may encounter in life, if we have faith in the Mystic Law and chant Nam-myoho-renge-kyo, we will inevitably enjoy peace of mind at the moment of death. Further, based on their dedicated practice of Buddhism, loved ones can create a bond that transcends life and death. On this issue, Nichiren wrote: "Those who practice this sutra [the Lotus Sutra]...will betake themselves to the same place, Eagle Peak. Moreover, as your deceased father believed in the Lotus Sutra along with you, he will definitely be reborn in the same place with you in the next life."[10]

The noted Indian Buddhist theoretician Vasubandhu proclaimed that the dead could not spontaneously change their karmic effects during the intermediate existence. But Nichiren taught that prayers offered by the living could mitigate the sufferings of the deceased and affect the conditions of their rebirth. This, according to Nichiren, is because prayers based on the state of Buddhahood transcend life and death; prayers are "transmitted" to the deceased, enabling them to enter a joyful state as a result of prayer on their behalf.

Nam-myoho-renge-kyo, the Mystic Law, permeates every living being and every phenomenon in the universe. The birth and death of living beings, the occurrence and cessation of nonliving phenomena and the constant flux of the universe are all manifestations of this Law. The Law enables our lives to continue eternally from one existence to the next. If we have faith in and practice the Mystic Law, we will come to realize that our own lives are eternal.

Life After Death

Nichiren described the state of a person who continues chanting Nam-myoho-renge-kyo until the moment of death, and who thereby establishes Buddhahood within:

For one who summons up one's faith and chants

Nam-myoho-renge-kyo with the profound insight that now is the last moment of one's life, the sutra proclaims: "When the lives of these persons come to an end, they will be received into the hands of a thousand Buddhas, who will free them from all fear and keep them from falling into the evil paths of existence." How can we possibly hold back our tears at the inexpressible joy of knowing that not just one or two, not just one hundred or two hundred, but as many as a thousand Buddhas will come to greet us with open arms![11]

In another writing, Nichiren expanded on this:

Even if someone were to cut off our heads with a saw, impale our bodies with lances, or shackle our feet and bore them through with a gimlet, as long as we are alive, we must keep chanting Nam-myoho-renge-kyo, Nam-myoho-renge-kyo. Then, if we chant until the very moment of death, Shakyamuni, Many Treasures, and the Buddhas of the ten directions will come to us instantly, exactly as they promised during the ceremony at Eagle Peak. Taking our hands and bearing us on their shoulders, they will carry us to Eagle Peak. The two sages, the two heavenly kings, and the ten demon daughters will guard us, while all the heavenly gods and benevolent deities will raise a canopy over our heads and unfurl banners on high. They will escort us under their protection to the treasure land of Tranquil Light. How can such joy possibly be described![12]

In both of these passages, Nichiren mentions the countless Buddhas who will greet us the moment we die. This was to convince his contemporaries, who deeply respected the Buddhas, of the greatness of his teaching. Analyzing the texts more carefully, however, we can see that phrases such as "a thousand Buddhas" and "Shakyamuni, Many Treasures, and the Buddhas of the ten directions" refer, in fact, to the Buddhahood inherent in our own lives and the universe itself. Nichiren was actually saying that people who believe in and chant Nam-myoho-renge-kyo will enjoy the benefits of peace and serenity, even in death, because they have harmonized with the universal Buddha nature that permeates, at the most fundamental level, life and the vast universe.

In a letter to a believer, he elaborated on this theme:

> And when you are happy, you should remember that your happiness in this life is nothing but a dream within a dream, and that the only true happiness is that found in the pure land of Eagle Peak, and with that thought in mind, chant Nam-myoho-renge-kyo. Continue your practice without backsliding until the final moment of your life, and when that time comes, behold! When you climb the mountain of perfect enlightenment and gaze around you in all directions, then to your amazement you will see that the entire realm of phenomena is the Land of Tranquil Light. The ground will be of lapis lazuli, and the eight paths will be set apart by golden ropes. Four kinds of flowers will fall from the heavens, and music will resound in the air. All Buddhas and bodhisattvas will be present in complete joy, caressed by the breezes of eternity, happiness, true self, and purity. The time is fast approaching when we too will count ourselves among their number. But if we are weak in faith, we will never reach that wonderful place. [13]

When he used images and concepts of an ideal world, such as the pure land of Eagle Peak or the Land of Tranquil Light,

Nichiren was referring to eternal life. In some schools of Buddhism, attaining nirvana implies the cessation of transmigration among the six paths and the end of life itself. According to Mahayana Buddhism, however, even after achieving Buddhahood one will, very soon after death, reappear in the physical world, taking the form of an ordinary mortal in order to work for the salvation of others. The time that it takes for a life to pass through the intermediate stage between death and rebirth depends upon the condition of that individual's life. If, on dying, a life enters universal Buddhahood, it takes very little time before it is reborn into this world.

The "time" required before an individual life is reborn is different from that which we experience in this world: it is time as sensed by that particular life, a duration that will vary according to the individual's spiritual state. To use a familiar analogy, if we are extremely happy, time flies by, so that an hour may seem more like a minute; conversely, if we are suffering, time drags its feet so that a minute seems like an hour.

The Ten Worlds also exist in the great life of the universe. If one's state of life at the last moment is that of the world of Hell, then that person's life fuses with the world of Hell in the universal life; if one is in Heaven, that person's life fuses with the world of Heaven. In other words, the person's life merges with the world in the universal life whose "wavelength" matches it.

As to the manner in which our lives fuse with the universe, even though we speak of the Ten Worlds inherent in the universal life, they do not exist as actual places somewhere in the universe. For example, the world of Heaven is not out there next to Venus. Rather, the Ten Worlds permeate the entirety of the universal life. Whether we are speaking of the world of Hell, the world of Heaven or the world of Buddhahood, each pervades the entire universe.

When, at death, our lives become one with the respective state—Hell, Heaven and so on—in the universal life, we become one with the entire universe. For precisely this reason, as long as the appropriate external cause exists, there is no restriction on when and where in the universe we can appear. We are reborn with the body and mind and in the environment most suited to us.

Regarding those who have realized Buddhahood, Nichiren wrote:

> One cherishes and profoundly awakens to the truth [of life], and is in accordance with the will of all Buddhas through-out time. He receives the protection of the two saints, the two heavenly gods and the Ten Goddesses, and without impediment attains rebirth in the supreme Land of Tranquil Light. In a moment he returns to the realm of dreams in which he repeats the cycle of birth and death in the Nine Worlds. His body [of the Law] pervades the lands in the ten directions, and his mind enters the lives of all sentient beings. He urges from within and induces from without, appropriately combining the two [to lead people to enlight-enment]. Harmonizing internal and external causes, he employs his infinite power of compassion in order to widely benefit living beings.[14]

Nichiren taught that, as people escape from the vicious cir-cle of birth and death in the six paths, they will simultaneously commence the bodhisattva's work of leading others to salva-tion, undergoing innumerable cycles of birth and death in the process. Therefore, to bodhisattvas, birth and death are the cause of Buddhahood, not of suffering, and the means whereby they work for the benefit of others.

Death with Dignity

Buddhism establishes three categories of pain: physical, psychological and existential. Death is said to be the conjunction of these three. The first type of pain can be alleviated with the help of medical science. Social welfare systems and the combined cooperative efforts of family and the medical system can lighten psychological suffering.

Overcoming existential suffering, however, is another matter. This is the anguish caused by the idea of our own mortality. Belief in eternal life provides a way of thinking about life and death and of triumphing over the fear and apprehension of death. If people can internalize a spiritual view of life and death, it will empower them to overcome the despair of these three types of pain and greet the final chapter of their lives tranquil and fulfilled.

Advances in modern medicine greatly prolong the predeath period for patients in the terminal phase of their illness. Consequently, one main concern of contemporary medicine is to find ways to support the dying so they can overcome fear and anxiety. This is why terminal care has become a focus of great attention.

In cases of incurable illness, as the end draws near, people wish to maintain their pride, self-respect and some control over their faculties and personal dignity. There is certainly growing awareness of patients' rights, including the right to die. Without the possibilities offered today by medical science, this right would be purely theoretical. Medical science has made great progress in developing treatments that relieve pain and eliminate the agony of illness. Life is greatly prolonged through sophisticated technology. The downside of these advances, however, is when they maintain patients in an irrevocably vegetative state. From this comes the moral question: Does a comatose or nearly comatose patient with no hope of recovery, attached to an artificial respirator, feeding tubes and various other machines, possess true human dignity?

Dying with dignity is an integral part of each human being's responsibility. Human life is dignified in and of itself, a truth to be respected by the patient, within the family and throughout society. It only follows, then, that the doctor–patient relationship must be founded on mutual respect. Today, however, it is extremely difficult to define that dignity in relationships dominated by technologies that far outstrip advances in medical ethics. It is vital that we carefully examine all the issues surrounding the dignified death of people only kept alive by artificial means.

My mentor, Josei Toda, died with dignity. From his sickbed, he encouraged others and answered questions about Buddhism. Until his last breath, he gave advice to people in distress. All his life, he radiated health in the true sense of the word, even after he became ill. True health does not mean the absence of illness. Rather, it is a life-state characterized by openness to the hearts and minds of others and to the environment. It is a constant readiness to exercise the creative ability to serve society.

Violent or Accidental Death

On September 11, 2001, thousands of people lost their lives in a way that deeply affected millions of people. I heard the news with great shock and sorrow, and prayed for the victims, recalling a passage from the Lotus Sutra: "Now this threefold world is all my [Shakyamuni's] domain, and the living beings in it are all my children. Now this place is beset by many pains and trials. I am the only person who can rescue and protect others."[15]

A passenger on one of the hijacked airliners was a Nichiren Buddhist and a friend of mine. His family, all of whom practice

Nichiren Buddhism, have written to me and reported that, while originally shattered by the tragedy, they have since confronted the situation face to face and used it to deepen their faith and further strengthen their lives.

Believers in the Mystic Law do not necessarily live long lives untouched by disaster. Death is a certainty. Therefore, it's not whether our lives are long or short, but whether, while alive, we form a connection with the Mystic Law—the eternal elixir for all life's ills. That, in retrospect, determines whether we have lived the best possible lives. When we strive continually to reveal our Buddha nature and to embrace others with the compassion of a bodhisattva, whatever we face in life then becomes fuel for our enlightenment. Disasters are then never merely disasters, and even a short life can be as fruitful as a long one. With faith, we can find infinite meaning in each event whether good or bad.

Buddhism elucidates that life's adversities play a role in eradicating the negative effects of an individual's karma. In this connection, we should note the brutal disaster that Shakyamuni himself suffered during the later years of his life when King Virudhaka of Kosala commanded the massacre of the Shakya tribe. Although historical accounts differ, it seems that the Shakya tribe was virtually annihilated at Virudhaka's behest. The massacre is counted as one of the nine great ordeals experienced by the Buddha.

Several of Shakyamuni's most eminent disciples also suffered greatly in the course of their Buddhist practice. During the Buddha's lifetime, Devadatta beat the Buddhist nun Utpalavarna to death after she reproached him for attempting to crush the Buddha with a boulder dropped from the top of Eagle Peak. While practicing religious mendicancy in Rajagriha, Maudgalyayana, reputedly the foremost Buddhist disciple in the sphere of transcendental powers, was murdered by what was essentially a lynch mob. Nevertheless, even though Shakyamuni personally experienced considerable ordeals, and even though his followers were persecuted, he continued to teach people how to free themselves from suffering, so that gradually they would be led along the path to Buddhahood. Thanks to Shakyamuni's determination to spread his teachings despite obstacles and tragedy, Buddhism was for a time widely revered in India and China and eventually became a world religion.

Death of the Spirit

The Nirvana Sutra says: "Bodhisattvas, have no fear in your hearts because of such things as wild elephants. But evil friends — they are what you should fear! If you are killed by a wild elephant, you will not fall into any of the three evil paths. But if evil friends lead you to your death, you are certain to fall into one of them."[16]

The meaning of this passage is that, so long as we live in human society, we cannot avoid suffering. However, even if an unexpected accident — symbolized here by wild elephants — were to cause our death, we would not fall into the evil paths. By contrast, if we are swayed by negative influences and give up seeking to improve our lives and help others, thereby abandoning the road to Buddhahood, we shall, according to the sutra, fall into the three lower worlds — Hell, Hunger and Animality.

Buddhism thus distinguishes between the death of our body and the death of our spirit, our self-motivated pursuit of the path of Buddhahood. In terms of the Buddhist idea of eternal life, physical death has no direct bearing on true happiness. Rather, so long as we maintain the practice of Buddhist principles during our lifetime, we can minimize the duration of our intermediate existence and be swiftly reborn into this world and continue along the path of Buddhist practice. The ultimate frightful thing from the standpoint of Buddhism, then, is not physical death but the death in our hearts of the quest for the Law.

Life and Death Are Immanent in the Eternal

Shakyamuni regarded his own death as a means to an end, as it assisted him in his primary aim: the salvation of all people. He explained to his followers that, were he to remain forever in this world, people would rely on him rather than on their own faculties. Therefore, he taught, the Buddha would not remain in this world in perpetuity but would come and go at intervals. He therefore urged people instead to seek the Buddha's compassion, wisdom and mercy through his teachings and through their own diligence.

Every individual's death is, likewise, a means to an end — that is, a means to rebirth. As we grow older, we become weak and sickly and eventually die. But we do not die for nothing; we die to start a new life. The fundamental purpose of death, then, is birth — to allow us to start fresh in the next phase of our eternal life cycle.

The inscription on a bronze tablet that was hung on the wall of the bedroom of the house where Leonardo da Vinci, the genius who epitomized the Renaissance, was believed to have died, casts death in a poetic light: "A full life is long, a full day brings sound sleep, and an accomplished life brings a tranquil death." Leonardo's assertion strikes a sympathetic chord with the Buddhist teaching that death is but an expedient means — that life continues. Our day begins with an invigorating awakening. And at night we lay our tired bodies down for their much-deserved rest. Refreshed by sleep, we wake again the next morning with renewed energy. In terms of life's eternity, we can view death as the first step of the journey to a new existence.

The sixteenth chapter of the Lotus Sutra tells us, "There is no ebb or flow of birth and death."[17] Nichiren interpreted this sentence as follows:

> Regarding life and death with abhorrence and trying to separate oneself from them is delusion, or partial enlightenment. To clearly perceive life and death as the essence of eternal life is realization, or total enlightenment. Now Nichiren and his disciples who chant Nam-myoho-renge-kyo awaken to the ebb and flow of birth and death as the innate workings of life that is eternal.[18]

This passage expands on one of the profoundest Buddhist doctrines, the view that birth and death are inherent in eternal life. This means that our lives were brought into being neither by some transcendent god nor by the actions of our parents, but that they have always existed within the universe. "Eternal life" here signifies that our lives have continued and will continue to exist eternally with the universe — they have neither beginning nor end, and their existence is not intermittent but continuous. Apart from birth and death, there can be no eternal life.

If we correctly perceive birth and death as intrinsic workings of eternal life, as Nichiren teaches, we proceed from delusion to awakening. Put another way, we move from the superficial view that we become Buddhas after freeing ourselves from birth and death to the profound understanding that Buddhahood is inherent in us always within the cycle of birth and death, not apart from it. By basing our lives on this understanding, we will then have no fear of the sufferings of birth and death. Instead, we can accumulate treasures of boundless value within our lives so that, eternally and joyously, we will repeat the cycle of birth and death.

Nature, society, our own daily affairs—clearly all three are in constant flux, never remaining in the same state and continually repeating the cycle of birth and death. When we perceive that the life of the individual coexists with the universe and that birth and death are alternating aspects of a life that is eternal, we come to understand our own lives and the lives of those around us, as well as the world as a whole. We discover within us a "self" unaffected by the changing realities of human life and society, and this discovery enables us to overcome our fear of death. There is nothing more wonderful for a human being than to attain this state of life.

Implications for Our Present Lifetime

We have examined at some length the Buddhist view of eternal life. But what is the value of these theories for the living? Unless our ideas concerning death have some bearing on the way we conduct ourselves in this lifetime, they are merely speculation on a subject that affects every one of us on the most intimate level. The issue of death demands that we make continued efforts to understand it.

Among those who believe life is a one-time proposition, we commonly find both hedonists and pessimists. In general, the hedonist believes that since death is final, we should seek as much pleasure as possible before it occurs. The pessimist argues that even life's pleasures are too fleeting to be satisfactory; therefore, death is ultimately preferable to life.

There are those who, though rejecting the idea of an afterlife, attempt to make their present lives as worthwhile and noble as possible. Some people devote themselves to work they believe will contribute to the good of humankind. Others strive for a type of immortality by creating works that survive their own passing.

While some who maintain no faith in eternity may indeed realize specific spiritual goals, it is difficult for the great majority to do so. Ordinary mortals are inclined either to try putting the fear of death out of their minds or to turn to any expedient in hopes of forestalling it. Philosophies that promise people a full and meaningful life in the present, even though they believe in no life to come, are to be valued; but they usually cannot do much for those dominated by the dread of dying.

As for the common belief that immortality means being reborn in some heavenly realm, it seems doubtful that any creed of this sort can really enrich a person's life on earth. The opposite is more likely the case, because the hope for a future paradise often inspires resignation in the face of life's difficulties.

Particularly objectionable to Buddhism is the idea that all living beings undergo an eternal fixed cycle of transmigration — in other words, a man is always reborn as a man, and a dog as a dog, and no matter what these beings do, they can never change their fundamental destiny. The Buddhist theory of cause and effect refutes such thinking.

It is a mistake to describe transmigration as a closed circuit within a single place. We must think of it as a three-dimensional, open cycle — a spiral that may lead upward or downward. As life undergoes the eternal repetitions of birth and death, it expands freely and dynamically, always charged with limitless potential for self-improvement.

Living organisms eternally go back and forth between life and death, which are themselves but two phases of existence. The causes a person forms in the present manifest as effects in the future. By applying this simple law to our lives, we can develop a constructive, hopeful attitude toward our daily activities and recognize the true value of life in this present world. The future does not exist apart from the present, nor will it remain fixed in a single plane. What and how we will be in lives to come depend on what we do now. Every thought and every act play a role in shaping our future, both in life and death. The law of causality is valid for every life, because it permeates and molds the great, eternal flow of cosmic life.

What, then, are the practical implications of this philosophy? How should it affect our conduct and attitudes?

First, it provides us with the courage to face both life and death. It enables us to see death not as some terrifying unknown but as a normal phase of existence that alternates with life in an eternal cycle.

Second, it teaches us to treasure the life we now live and to make it as worthwhile as possible. If we believe in our heart that present behavior creates and determines future existences, we will strive to cultivate ourselves and make the most of what each day offers.

Third, it teaches us that the only way to fulfill the potential of the human race is to live just, kind, benevolent and compassionate lives — to be aware that each activity in which we engage can be the source of growth and self-reformation. It is comforting to know that the good fortune we amass through our conduct is undiminished by death, that it is integral to life and will enhance our eternal self.

Finally, this way of thinking enables us to redirect our instinctive desires so that we can elevate our state of being. We learn to avoid the pitfalls of hedonism and pessimism, to find joy and truth in compassion rather than in an ephemeral hope for rebirth in paradise.

Those familiar only with the ascetic traditions of early Buddhism may see Buddhism as pessimistic or nihilistic — something designed only to prepare people for death. In fact, Mahayana all human beings how to enjoy lives of complete fulfillment. Far from being negative, Buddhism affirms and exalts life. That's because the Buddhist philosophy of eternal life is not an expedient designed to persuade people to accept their mortality; it is a realistic and unfailing view of life established through myriad struggles against the sufferings of birth, aging, sickness and death. It teaches us to face the harsh realities of life with conviction and hope; it enjoins us to devote all our actions and thoughts to the welfare of others, because compassion is the ultimate source of cosmic life. By cherishing this philosophy, we can turn each difficulty into a source of power that brings joy to our lives.

Looking Ahead

Montaigne said, "To philosophize is to learn to die." Similarly, Buddhism teaches us: "First learn about death, and then about other matters." As both statements suggest, learning about death enriches life.

How we perceive the meaning of death and the meaning of life hinges completely on whether we can establish a correct view of life and death. Goethe says, "Those who have no hope of another life are already dead in this one."[19]

We study Buddhism to live vibrantly and with eternal hope. Will death, which inevitably comes to each of us, be a time of dignity and honor? Or will we end in pitiful demise? This is completely reliant on how we live our lives right now, today. In that sense, the moment of death truly exists in the present. This leads us to our next chapter, which examines the boundless potential of a single moment of life.

CHAPTER FIVE

Life's Unlimited Potential

Problems, as we have seen, are not in themselves the fundamental cause of unhappiness. Lack of power and wisdom to solve them is the real cause. Fortunately we all innately possess infinite power and wisdom; and Buddhism shows us how to develop these qualities.

When in the depths of despair or grappling with a difficult problem, it may be hard to believe that our lives possess unlimited potential. But this is the essence of one of the profoundest Buddhist teachings, known as "three thousand realms in a single moment of life," which we will explore in this chapter.

A Comprehensive View of Life

The development of Western scientific civilization has been bolstered—perhaps even dominated—by humanism, a doctrine emphasizing the superiority of humans as rational beings. But humanism has not always been grounded in a comprehensive view of life. Ultimately, the attitude that human beings are the center of the universe is narrow and egocentric. While a sense of self or ego is necessary for a fulfilling life, attachment to the idea of self as the whole of existence is limited and even dangerous according to Buddhism. Buddhism teaches that liberation from suffering lies in our awakening to the far broader life beyond the finite self.

Our worldview is shaped by our consciousness of self. Perceiving that the universe is divided into self and other — internal and external — arises from our consciousness of self. This consciousness likewise gives rise to other dualities: for example, the duality of mind and body, in which we regard the mind as the true self whereas the body somehow is not; the duality of the material and the spiritual; and the duality of humankind and nature. Modern civilization's evolution under such dualistic thinking is also the root of many of our present conflicts.

Buddhism teaches that our lives are not limited to what we ordinarily perceive as the self but encompass other people, the world and even the universe. Perhaps nowhere do we find a better exposition of this idea than in the teaching of three thousand realms in a single moment of life, which elucidates the unlimited potential of our lives. Several key Buddhist principles — such as the oneness of body and mind and the oneness of life and its environment — derive from this teaching. Because the "three thousand realms" teaching places dualities into a larger context, one that harmonizes apparent opposites, understanding it can help solve problems that arise from dualistic thinking.

The philosophical system of "three thousand realms" was developed in China by T'ien-t'ai, the outstanding Buddhist theoretician of the sixth century. This system, based on the Lotus Sutra, comprises a worldview that explains the mutually inclusive relationship of all phenomena and the ultimate reality of life. This means that the life of Buddhahood is universally inherent in all beings, and the distinction between a common person and a Buddha exists on the level of phenomena. In Japanese, three thousand realms in a single moment of life is known as *ichinen sanzen*. A literal translation of *ichinen* is "one thought" or "one mind," and it denotes the true aspect or ulti-mate reality that arises at each moment in our ordinary lives. *Sanzen*, meaning "three thousand," refers to the multitude of unvarying laws governing phenomena through which the ulti-mate reality is manifested.

The figure of three thousand is derived from a multiplication of component principles of *ichinen sanzen*(which will be dis-cussed in detail later in this chapter): the Ten Worlds, or states of life, in which each world possesses the other nine in addi-tion to itself, thus representing one hundred worlds in all; the ten factors with which each of these hundred worlds is endowed, giving us one thousand factors in all; and the three realms of existence in which each of these thousand factors operate. And so we arrive at our total of three thousand.

While the "three thousand realms" principle is a detailed and complex analysis of each moment of life, Nichiren believed that everyone was capable of grasping this concept, which he summarized or condensed as the phrase *Nam-myoho-renge-kyo*. Through studying the "three thousand realms" principle, we can better understand the philosophical and cultural background of Nichiren's teachings and also see why chanting Nam-myoho-renge-kyo is a powerful Buddhist practice.

The "three thousand realms" principle reveals that all phe-nomena, without exception, exist within each moment of an individual's life, and that every such moment therefore has infi-nite potential.

Nichiren explained that an individual's life at each moment simultaneously permeates the entire universe and encompasses within itself all the laws and phenomena of the universe. There-fore, a person's life is literally coextensive with the universe. Three thousand realms in a single moment of life provides a conceptual framework to express this point.

THE THREE THOUSAND REALMS

Comes from the following calculation:

10 (Ten Worlds) X 10 (Ten Worlds) X 10 (Ten Factors) X 3 (Three Realms)

Life at any moment manifests one of the Ten Worlds. Each of these worlds possesses the potential for all ten within itself; this "mutual possession" represents a hundred possible worlds.

Each of these hundred worlds possesses ten factors, making one thousand factors or potentials, and these operate within the three realms, thus making three thousand realms.

Eternity and Buddhahood Exist in the Moment

The physical world continually shows us that even infinitesimally small things contain vast potential. Physicists largely believe that the entire universe originated in an almost indescribably small "cosmic egg," perhaps the size of a subatomic particle. The fusion of minuscule nuclei can produce the immense energy of the hydrogen bomb. Hundreds of millions of units of information are stored in a gene too small to see through a microscope. And the human brain is believed to contain about fifteen billion cells called neurons, each of which spreads its dendrites to make up to ten thousand connections (synapses) with other neurons. Because of this network of almost incomprehensible scale, we can say that the potential of the human brain is virtually limitless.

In terms of time, life at each moment might be thought of as a cross section of a continuum stretching from the infinite past into the infinite future. Think of a person's life-moment as being like a television picture. In the space of a second, thirty successive still images flash across the television screen, merging to form a coherent, apparently moving picture. But the length of a moment as defined in the Buddhist scriptures would be far shorter than the duration of one of these images. *The Great Commentary on the Abhidharma* says that there are "sixty-five moments in a single snap of the fingers"; a moment in Buddhism, therefore, is almost inconceivably brief. An individual lifetime is an accumulation of such minuscule moments that flow from the past through the present into the future. Because eternity is an unbroken string of these moments—and because each moment is considered the condensation of an entire lifetime— our condition of life at each moment is of supreme importance as it determines the overall course of our lives. Learning to master each moment, then, becomes of paramount concern.

One of the ten honorific titles given to the Buddha is "Thus Come One" (Tathagata, in Sanskrit), meaning a person who has arrived from the world of truth. Thus Come One also means "one who emerges from the truth moment by moment," and it indicates that in every moment the Buddha manifests the ultimate truth. Further, Thus Come One, or Buddha, can mean the ultimate reality manifesting itself as the phenomenal world in every moment. Although the moment recedes with the flow of time, life at each moment transcends the temporal framework; each moment encompasses the ultimate reality, which remains unchanging throughout past, present and future. This, of course, is far beyond the ordinary bounds of our comprehension.

Josei Toda, when discussing this teaching, often cited a passage of the Immeasurable Meanings Sutra, a prologue to the Lotus Sutra, which reads: "The entity is neither existence nor nonexistence; neither cause nor circumstance; neither itself nor another; neither square nor round; neither short nor long;

neither rising nor falling; neither birth nor death; neither creation nor appearance, nor artificial;...neither blue nor yellow, nor red nor white; neither scarlet nor purple, nor any other color."

This collection of negatives is meant to show that the ultimate reality is beyond our powers of description and conception. We can observe our physical and mental activities to a certain extent through disciplines such as biology, biochemistry, physiology and psychology. But all these sciences deal with phenomena that are mere expressions of life, not life itself. The ultimate reality of life is intangible and invisible, unconstrained by time and space, yet it manifests as the phenomenal world in every moment.

We are subject to change both physically and mentally. Our physical bodies are composed of many millions of cells that are constantly dying and being replaced. Our minds, too, change, as various emotions and thoughts occur. As time flows by, we continually repeat the cycle of death and rebirth. The constantly changing circumstances of our bodies and minds are considered to be the inherent workings of a fundamentally unchanging reality. The Buddhist worldview extends beyond limited descriptions of birth and death. It encompasses a changeless and eternal truth expressed in all things—self and other, tangible and intangible, sentient and insentient. It alternately manifests as the active phase called "life" and recedes into the latent phase called "death."

To illuminate this view of life, Toda often quoted from the sixteenth chapter of the Lotus Sutra:

> In order to save living beings,
> as an expedient means I appear to enter into nirvana
> but in truth I do not pass into extinction.
> I am always here, preaching the Law.[1]

In other words, the Buddha's death, an expression of his great compassion, inspires people to seek to establish their own Buddhahood, yet the ultimate reality that the Buddha has realized —Buddhahood—is eternal and unchanging.

Another passage from this chapter, which helps us further see beyond impermanence and into the realm of the eternal, reads: "The Thus Come One perceives the true aspect of the threefold world exactly as it is. There is no ebb or flow of birth and death, and there is no existing in this world and later entering extinction."[2] The "true aspect" actually encompasses both the eternal and the changing: birth and death are inherent workings of life, which is eternal. Toda explained this view by applying the above quotation to our individual lives, saying:

> Nirvana, that is, our death, is a means to our rebirth. With age, we are destined to become weak and sickly, and, eventually, to die. At death, our physical body will decay, but our life will merge back into the great life of the universe. In this latent state, it recharges with energy, so to speak, for its rebirth. In this way, we repeat the cycle of birth and death, based on the Law permeating all living beings and phenomena in the universe. Death, then, can be likened to the function of sleep. It is an expedient means to dispel our fatigue and rejuvenate our lives for our next existence.

Birth and death are thus natural expressions of the eternal reality of life, and this eternal reality is also the ever-changing phenomena of birth and death. Freedom from the suffering of change comes only at the moment we awaken to the timeless truth underlying each life-moment. Then, as Nichiren wrote, "We repeat the cycle of birth and death secure upon the earth of our inherent enlightened nature." Here, he referred to an eternally existing state of absolute freedom. "Secure upon the earth of our inherent enlightened nature" means undergoing life and death based on the supreme life of the Mystic Law.

Undergoing the cycle of life and death in the nine worlds means navigating one's way awkwardly through difficulties and hardships. It is like veering along a path strewn with potholes; sometimes we fall in and cannot get back on track; sometimes we have accidents and get injured. On the other hand, experiencing life in the world of Buddhahood is like driving a high-performance car on a smooth highway while enjoying the brilliant scenery around us.

Although the moments of our lives appear to flit by, from a deeper viewpoint, we can see that together they encompass the ultimate reality. Every individual moment transcends the bounds of space and time to be simultaneously one with the cosmic life force — the ultimate reality of the universe. All forms of life interrelate endlessly in the vast totality of cosmic life, and yet none of them ever loses its uniqueness. Nichikan, the noted eighteenth-century priest and scholar, expressed this idea:

> In light of the Lotus Sutra, the phrase "three thousand realms in a single moment of life" has two meanings: to include and to permeate. On the one hand, the entire universe is included in each moment, and on the other, each moment permeates the entire universe. Each moment is a particle of dust that possesses the elements of all lands in the universe, or a drop of water whose essence differs in no way from the vast ocean itself.

Let us turn now to the relationships that exist among each moment's component principles. These are the Ten Worlds, their mutual possession, the ten factors and the three realms.

The Ten Worlds

The first component of the "three thousand realms" principle is the principle of the Ten Worlds, which illuminates the states or conditions of our lives at any given moment. T'ien-t'ai wrote, "Life at each moment is endowed with the Ten Worlds," meaning that in every moment of life there exists the potential for ten conditions: Hell, Hunger, Animality, Anger, Humanity, Heaven, Learning, Realization, Bodhisattva and Buddhahood. This theory describes the subjective sensations experienced by the self at the most fundamental level. At one time, it was thought that these were ten distinct and separate places into which people were reborn and that the particular place was determined by the nature of the individual's accumulated karmic effects. In Nichiren Buddhism, however, the Ten Worlds are viewed not as physical locations but as life-states inherent in each of us.

Hell:
First, there is the world of **Hell**. This comes from the Sanskrit term *naraka*, which literally means underground prison. A variant of this term, *naraku*, survives in the modern Japanese expression "to fall into the abyss." The Japanese word equivalent of Hell is composed of two characters meaning "earth" and "prison." Earth means the lowest place; and prison indicates being shackled and totally immobilized.

Hell is the most miserable state, one in which a person is bound hand and foot by suffering. While there are many gradations in the world of Hell, it is a state in which life is painful; where anything you see only makes you feel miserable. Those in this state have an extremely weak life force.

Nichiren wrote, "Rage is the world of hell."³ Anger and rage

TEN WORLDS

Ten potential states or conditions a person can manifest or experience.

Hell

Hunger
(hungry spirits)   **THREE EVIL PATHS**

                        FOUR EVIL PATHS

Animality
(animals)

                                              SIX PATHS

Anger
(*asuras*)

Humanity
(human beings)

Heaven
(heavenly beings)

Learning
(voice-hearers)

                        THE TWO VEHICLES

Realization
(cause-awakened
ones)   **THE FOUR
                                NOBLE WORLDS**

Bodhisattva

Buddhahood

THE NINE WORLDS

become sources of further self-destruction. Anger, as explained earlier, is one of the Three Poisons. Those who are suffering—whether due to family discord, sickness or the flames of jealousy—and whose hearts swirl with rage at whatever has brought on that suffering, cannot recognize that the actual cause for the suffering exists in their own lives. Some people direct the rage at themselves and their inability to do anything about the suffering. We could describe this impotent rage as the despairing groan of a life that has exhausted every possible avenue.

Hunger:

Next is the world of **Hunger,** or hungry spirits. Hunger derives from the Sanskrit word *preta*, which originally meant the deceased. In Buddhism, the term came to signify a realm of misery, like Hell, into which dead people might fall. *Preta* also means ancestral spirit. In India, it was thought that many ancestral spirits were hungry and desirous of food, which is perhaps why the dead came to be referred to as hungry spirits.

Hunger is a condition governed by endless appetites—for food, profit, pleasure, power, recognition or fame. It is a state in which one is never truly satisfied. Nichiren explained that the world of Hunger is characterized by greed, another of the Three Poisons. Those in the world of Hunger become slaves to their desires, which prevents them from feeling inner freedom and produces suffering.

People's desires are limitless. There is the fundamental desire to live, the instinctual desire for food, the materialistic desire for possessions, the psychological desire to have attention. We could not live without desires. In many cases, desires become the energy with which we advance and realize self-improvement. That's why it is said of the world of Hunger, "This path is connected with other paths and leads to both good and evil."[4]

The real issue, therefore, is how we use desire. Those in Hunger do not use desire to create value; instead, pulled this way and that, they suffer and cause injury to others.

Animality:

Third, the world of **Animality**—also referred to as the world of animals—is a condition driven by instinct. Ruled by the law of the jungle, people in this state fear the strong but despise and prey upon those weaker than themselves. They lack reason, morality or wisdom with which to control themselves and are therefore so caught up in their immediate circumstances that they lose sight of the underlying principles that govern all things. Nichiren explained that the world of Animality is characterized by foolishness, the third of the Three Poisons.

When people lack a sound standard for judging good and evil, a firm moral or ethical foundation, they act instinctively and without shame. We might say that those in this state, while human, have lost their humanity. According to Dostoevsky: "People talk sometimes of bestial cruelty, but that's a great injustice and insult to the beasts; a beast can never be so cruel as a man, so artistically cruel."[5]

The worlds of Hell, Hunger and Animality are collectively known as the three evil paths

Anger:

The name of the fourth world, **Anger**, derives from the Sanskrit term *asura*. In ancient India, *asura* originally represented a class of benevolent deities. But in later mythology, they came to be regarded as belligerent demons that ceaselessly fight with gods.

The world of Anger is characterized by perversity, by having a mind that is fawning and crooked, as in the case of someone who hides his or her true feelings while making a false show of loyalty. This state, which is dominated by ego, is sometimes called the world of animosity because it is characterized by persistent, though not necessarily overt, aggressiveness. Compelled by the need to be superior to others, people in the state of Anger may feign politeness and even flatter others while inwardly despising them.

Anger is fundamentally an arrogant state of life. People in Anger are attached to the illusory assumption that they are better than others and direct their energy toward sustaining and enhancing this image. To ensure that others think of them in similarly glowing terms, they can never reveal their true feelings. Instead, they act obsequiously while a burning desire to surpass all others is their exclusive focus. With their inner feelings and outward appearance out of accord, they don't speak from the heart.

This is generally more sophisticated behavior than that of people in Hell, Hunger or Animality. Outwardly, people in Anger conduct themselves as virtuous people of benevolence, justice, propriety, wisdom and fidelity, trying to convince others that these are their true qualities. They may even come to believe their own virtuousness, deluding themselves that they are better than others because they are "so humble."

Buddhism teaches that the heart is most important. Of two people making comparable efforts, the results will differ greatly if one person is motivated by a value that transcends the self— good, beauty, the well-being of others—while the other is solely motivated by ego.

The worlds of Hell, Hunger, Animality and Anger are collectively called the four evil paths.

How can the tendency toward the world of Anger be overcome? This is the jumping-off point for entering the fifth world —Humanity, or human beings. Ultimately, when we learn to

channel the energy formerly directed toward winning over others into winning over ourselves, we enter the world of Humanity.

Humanity:

In **Humanity**, we strive to control our desires and impulses
through reason. We aspire for a higher state of life with the awareness that it is not the fact of our birth that makes us human beings,
it is only when we make tenacious effort to act in harmony with
our surroundings and other people that we are truly human.

Strictly speaking, the world of Humanity is the first step
toward attaining self-mastery, the culmination of which is to be
found in the worlds of Bodhisattva and Buddhahood, the ninth
and tenth worlds, respectively. In Sanskrit, a human being is
signified by the term *manusya*, which means one who thinks.
Accordingly, intellect is the key condition of Humanity. Without comparing themselves to others, people in Humanity follow
their own path.

In terms of the structure of the doctrine of the Ten Worlds,
Humanity is in the middle, just an increment above the four evil
paths. Nichiren repeatedly tells us that since we have had the
rare good fortune to be born as human beings, we should strive
to attain a still higher state of life. In Buddhism, the human body
is called the "correct vessel of the noble paths;" it is the vessel of
the Law for carrying out Buddhist practice. When we fill that
vessel with the great life of the world of Buddhahood, we realize the true significance of having been born as human beings.

Heaven:

The sixth world is that of **Heaven**. This state is characterized by
the intense joy or satisfaction we experience when, for example,
we obtain something material, physical or spiritual that we have
long desired, or when long-term suffering has finally been

relieved. Although it is intense, joy in this state is short-lived and extremely vulnerable to external influences.

The joy of Heaven is ephemeral like a mirage or a dream. A life spent in pursuit of a mirage is itself a mirage. The purpose of Buddhist practice is to establish an eternally indestructible state of happiness; not a fleeting happiness that perishes like a flower but an internal palace of happiness that will last throughout all time. This diamond palace, this treasure tower soaring to magnificent heights, is built through faith and practice.

These first six states, from Hell to Heaven, are collectively called the six paths, or the six lower worlds. All of them have in common one thing: they are brought about through either the fulfillment or the thwarting of various desires and impulses. Their appearance or disappearance is essentially governed by external circumstances. Most people spend their lives shuttling among these six states without ever realizing that they are completely at the mercy of their reactions to their environment. Any happiness or satisfaction gained in these states is tenuous. When trapped in the six lower worlds, we fail to realize this and instead base our happiness — indeed, the whole of our identity — on external factors, a mode in which we cannot transform our lives.

When we recognize that everything experienced in the six paths is impermanent, we begin a search for lasting truth. Through this quest, we enter the next two states, Learning and Realization. These two states, along with the ninth and tenth, Bodhisattva and Buddhahood, are named the four noble worlds. Unlike the six paths, which are characterized by attachment to self-centered desires, these four states are achieved only through deliberate and continued effort.

Learning:
In the seventh world, the state of **Learning**, we awaken to the impermanence of all things and the instability of the six paths. We dedicate ourselves to self-reformation and self-development by learning vicariously from others' ideas, knowledge and experience. This state is also referred to as the world of voice-hearers, which originally meant those who listened to the Buddha preach in person about the four noble truths and who practiced the eightfold path in order to acquire emancipation from earthly desires.

Realization:
The eighth is the world of **Realization,** or cause-awakened ones, and is characterized by individuals who arrive independently at an understanding of Buddhist truths. This state is similar to that of Learning, except that here people seek the truth not through others' teachings but through direct perception.

Together, the worlds of Learning and Realization are called the two vehicles. In these states, having realized the impermanence of all things, we win a measure of independence from attachment to the past and to our fixed notions. No longer are we merely subject to our environment; we seek to improve ourselves. We are willing to look squarely at the reality of death and seek the eternal, in contrast to those in the world of Heaven, who are distracted from life's harsh realities. On the downside, people of the two vehicles are more apt to pursue self-perfection than altruism.

Bodhisattva:
In contrast to the two vehicles, where people seek a theoretical understanding of the universal truth, the ninth world—**Bodhisattva**—is a state of compassion and altruistic behavior.

Although people in this state aspire to achieve supreme enlightenment themselves, at the same time they are determined that all other human beings, too, should reach the same understanding. Bodhisattva, a Sanskrit word that consists of *bodhi* (enlightenment) and *sattva* (being), means a person who seeks enlightenment while leading others to enlightenment as well. Conscious of the bonds that link us to everyone else, in the Bodhisattva state we realize that any happiness we enjoy alone is only partial and therefore illusory, and so we devote ourselves to alleviating others' suffering—even at the cost of our lives. As Nichiren stated: "Joy means that both oneself and others rejoice."[6]

The states from Hell to Bodhisattva are collectively known as the nine worlds, indicating the unenlightened condition of common mortals as contrasted with the Ten Worlds, which include Buddhahood.

Buddhahood:
The world of **Buddhahood**—the tenth world—is a state of infinite compassion, a total, incorruptible purity of life and absolute freedom in which we have the wisdom to recognize the ultimate reality of our lives. We achieve this state by manifesting our inherent Buddha nature. And, according to Buddhist teachings, only when we have established Buddhahood as our basis can we affect a reformation of our entire existence, directing all our physical and mental activities of the nine worlds toward altruistic and valuable goals.

Buddhahood, when viewed through the principle of the mutual possession of the Ten Worlds, however, is not a state removed from the sufferings and imperfections of ordinary people. Manifesting our Buddhahood does not mean we become special beings. We still continue working to defeat the negative functions of life and to transform all difficulties into causes for further development. Buddhahood is a state of complete access to the boundless wisdom, compassion, courage and other qualities inherent in life, a state in which we can create harmony with and among others and between ourselves and nature. Nichiren explained that Buddhahood is the most difficult life-state to demonstrate, but also wrote, "That ordinary people born in the latter age can believe in the Lotus Sutra is due to the fact that the world of Buddhahood is present in the human world."[7]

To give an analogy, if we liken dwelling in the nine worlds to being cooped up in a room, then dwelling in the world of Buddhahood would be like basking outdoors in the clear, bright sunshine. In the nine worlds, we are still part of the great macrocosm that is the world of Buddhahood. Though we vaguely sense this eternal aspect of our lives, because we are shut inside, surrounded by dense walls of illusion, we cannot fully comprehend our true environment. When, through faith, we break down these walls, we can freely enjoy the fresh air and sunshine of the Mystic Law pervading the universe. Then, there is no difference between being in the room and being outside.

There is something profound and mystic about the function of our state of life. How we perceive our lives — our impressions of the world around us, both spatially and temporally — will differ according to which of the Ten Worlds we are in. Whether we are aware of it, our state of life greatly determines our actions, thoughts, relationships and paths in life, as well as our emotions. State of life, moreover, is not only a property of individuals; a society, too, has a state of life.

Buddhism is unconcerned with ethnicity or race or level of schooling or social standing. Its gaze is trained directly on the condition of people's hearts, on their state of life. Power and influence do not make people great. The lives of many powerful people are ravaged by the worlds of Hunger and Animality. On the other hand, there are ordinary citizens who dwell in the joyous worlds of Bodhisattva and Buddhahood.

The compassion to strive to help people cultivate their inherent Buddhahood is key to the doctrine of the Ten Worlds.

Mutual Possession of the Ten Worlds

Nichiren wrote, "The doctrine of three thousand realms in a single moment of life begins with the concept of the mutual possession of the Ten Worlds."[8] The mutual possession of the Ten Worlds describes the dynamic structure of life in an all-embracing way. Mutual possession, or mutual inclusion, means that each of the Ten Worlds encompasses all of the other worlds within itself. We can interpret this to mean that all ten states are inherent in every individual; a person experiencing the world of Humanity one moment may, in the next, either remain in that state or manifest one of the other nine. Life, then, is not fixed in one of the ten conditions but at any moment can manifest any of them. Because of this principle, it is possible for us to change our state of life, for although we may "inhabit" a particular world, the other nine are always dormant in our lives. As Nichiren explained: "Even a heartless villain loves his wife and children. He too has a portion of the bodhisattva world within him."[9] Thus the state of Bodhisattva—like all the other states—exists even in the world of Hell.

Mutual possession explains how a state of life moves from dormancy to active manifestation, or from active manifestation back to dormancy. At one moment, for example, we may be experiencing the joy of Heaven, but our surroundings may suddenly change so that in the next moment we plunge into the depths of Hell. This does not mean that the Heaven within us has ceased to exist — it has simply shifted from a manifest state to a latent one and, with the appropriate external stimulus, will emerge again from dormancy. The ten states from Hell to Buddhahood, then, are activated by our relationship with the external world and are given expression in both the physical and spiritual aspects of our every activity. Although the Ten Worlds differ from one another, they have equal potential to shift from dormancy to activation and back again.

Which of the Ten Worlds will manifest at any given moment depends not only on external influences but also on one's basic tendencies. A particular external influence need not necessarily bring out the same world in two different people.

Of course, our conditions fluctuate from one moment to the next but, from a broader perspective, there is always one condition or set of conditions around which our activities revolve and to which we are most likely to revert. Some people's lives revolve around the three evil paths, some shuttle back and forth among the six lower worlds, and some people's primary motivation is the quest for the truth that characterizes the two vehicles.

The mutual possession of the Ten Worlds clarifies the fundamental equality and infinite potential of each human being. It implies that all individuals possess the potential to elevate their basic tendencies. Through continuing effort in Buddhist practice, we can gradually elevate our basic tendencies until we establish the supreme state of Buddhahood as our foundation. Buddhahood is not an abstract idea; it reveals itself tangibly in our daily behavior as human beings. Indeed, Buddhahood is our original nature, which, according to Nichiren, we can access through chanting Nam-myoho-renge-kyo.

During the process of elevating our basic tendencies, our perceptions and values are certain to change. Nichiren wrote: "Hungry spirits perceive the Ganges River as fire, human beings perceive it as water, and heavenly beings perceive it as amrita [divine nectar]. Though the water is the same, it appears differently according to one's karmic reward from the past."[10] He is saying that a life in the world of Hunger perceives the waters of the Ganges as if they were its own self-consuming flames of greed, whereas a life in a different state has a totally different perception. Although the passage refers only to perception in the states of Hunger, Humanity and Heaven, the principle obviously applies to all the other states as well. Thus, when we establish Buddhahood as our immutable foundation, we will be certain to create a life of limitless joy and absolute freedom.

In terms of the mutual possession of the Ten Worlds, attaining Buddhahood does not mean eradicating the lower nine worlds. Rather, it means making the best use of all of them. The mutual possession teaching, therefore, is very broad-minded.

Buddhist teachings that do not explain mutual possession treat the nine worlds with scorn, postulating that one can enter the world of Buddhahood only by eradicating the other nine. In effect, they try to carve away those parts of human existence that they regard as bad. They impose restriction and condemn shortcomings. This ultimately leads to the idea of annihilating one's consciousness and reducing one's body to ashes — in other words, to ridding oneself of earthly desires and attachments.

While self-reflection is of course important, if not done in a positive, growth-inspiring way, people's lives may become closed off and rigid, causing them to lose all sense of purpose.

A Japanese saying goes that trying to straighten the horns of a cow could kill the cow. Instead of nitpicking over others' weaknesses, it is far more valuable to encourage them, give them hope and enable them to find goals. Through doing so, we can help those who are impatient, for example, become those who cannot wait to take positive action.

This applies to one's personal growth as well as that of others. We can be completely ourselves. There is no need to appear to be what we are not. Since we are human, there will be times when we want to cry, times when we want to laugh, times when we are angry, as well as times when we are confused. Though we are ordinary people subject to such frailties, through Nichiren Buddhist practice, the world of Buddhahood can become our basic tendency in life. Then when anger is appropriate, we get angry. When suffering is needed, we suffer. When laughter is due, we laugh.

Nichiren wrote: "Suffer what there is to suffer, enjoy what there is to enjoy."[11] By leading such vigorous and vibrant lives, we can advance each day by leaps and bounds toward absolute happiness and help others do the same.

The Ten Factors

The next component of the three thousand realms is the principle of the ten factors, which provides a framework for analyzing aspects of life that remain constant within changing phenomena. While the Ten Worlds describe life's differing expressions, the ten factors clarify the aspects of existence that remain common to life in any state, from Hell to Buddhahood. Life in each of the Ten Worlds equally possesses the same ten factors. The ten factors principle also enables us to understand how life shifts from one of the Ten Worlds to another.

The Lotus Sutra lists the ten factors in this passage: "The true entity of all phenomena can only be understood and shared between Buddhas. This reality consists of appearance, nature, entity, power, influence, inherent cause, relation, latent effect, manifest effect, and their consistency from beginning to end."[12]

Since the ten factors are common to all life and phenomena, there can be no fundamental distinction between a Buddha and an ordinary person.

Appearance:
The first of the ten factors is **appearance**. It refers to attributes discernible from the outside, such as color, form, shape and behavior. In terms of human beings, appearance is the manifested, superficial side of our existence, such as the way we look, the body and its various functions.

Nature:
The second factor, **nature**, is the inherent nature, disposition or potential of a thing or being that is invisible from the outside. T'ien-t'ai characterized nature as unchanging and irreplaceable. The nature of fire, for instance, is unchanging and cannot be replaced by that of water. He also referred to a "true nature," which he regarded as the ultimate truth, or the Buddha nature. In terms of human existence, nature corresponds to such invisible or dormant qualities of life as mind and consciousness.

Entity:
The third factor is **entity**, the essence of life that permeates and integrates appearance and nature. Entity sustains one's individuality and manifests as both external appearance and internal nature but is in itself neither.

While these first three factors describe what life is, the next six factors describe life's dynamic functions.

Power:
Power, the fourth factor, refers to life's inherent capacity to act, its potential strength or energy to achieve something. As

TEN FACTORS

Patterns of existence common to all phenomena
in any of the Ten Worlds.

Appearance

Nature   } **DESCRIBE REALITY OF LIFE ITSELF**

Entity

Power

Influence

Internal Cause

Relation   } **DESCRIBE THE LAW OF CAUSE AND EFFECT**   } **DESCRIBE THE FUNCTIONS AND WORKINGS OF LIFE**

Latent Effect

Manifest Effect

Consistency from Beginning to End

examples, life in the world of Humanity has the power to
uphold ethical standards, and life in the world of Bodhisattva
has the power to relieve others' sufferings.

Influence:
The fifth factor, **influence**, represents the action produced when

life's inherent power is activated. Whether good or evil, influence is exerted in thought, speech or action.

Power and influence describe the workings of life in terms of space, while the others deal with causality and life's functions in terms of time. Power and influence presuppose the existence of some object toward which movement or action is directed. When accompanied by the dynamic factors of power and influence, entity can be thought of as an autonomous self that can act relative to other beings.

The next four factors explain how actions cause us to shift from one of the Ten Worlds to another.

Internal cause:
The sixth factor, **internal cause** is the cause latent in life that produces an effect of the same quality as itself, whether good, bad or neutral.

Relation:
Relation, the seventh factor, refers to the relationship of auxiliary causes to the internal cause. Auxiliary causes are various conditions, both internal and external, that trigger the internal cause to produce an effect. For example, a person who is hit seemingly without reason, may spontaneously become angry. The fact of being hit is an auxiliary cause, as might be the person's life tendency to easily get angry.

Latent effect:
Latent effect, the eighth factor, refers to the effect produced in life when an internal cause is activated through its relationship with various conditions. Anger that emerges from within after being hit is a good example of the latent effect.

Manifest effect:
Manifest effect, the ninth factor, means the tangible, perceivable result that eventually emerges as an expression of a latent effect.

These four factors—internal cause, relation, latent effect and manifest effect—all clarify the mechanism of cause and effect in a general sense.

Consistency from beginning to end:
Consistency from beginning to end is the tenth and unifying factor. It indicates that all previous nine factors from appearance to manifest effect are consistently and harmoniously interrelated. All nine factors thus consistently express the same life-state at any given moment. For example, people in the world of Hell have the dark and depressed appearance of those overwhelmed by suffering. Since their nature is filled with suffering and rage, their power and influence tend to mire those around them in darkness, too. They make the causes and receive the effects of Hell.

Those in the world of Heaven are typically bright and smiling in appearance. In their nature, since they feel uplifted, anything they see makes them happy. Their power and influence tend to make those around them feel buoyant and cheerful, too.

The eye of the Buddha perceives this true reality. The true reality of all phenomena is that each possesses latent potential (nature and power) and an openness to change (internal cause, relation, latent effect and manifest effect). Phenomena depend upon each other, are open to one another yet remain consistent and unified.

The factor of consistency from being to end can be viewed from a higher plane as well, from the perspective of the universal truth to which the Buddha became enlightened—namely, that as entities of the Mystic Law, the life of the Buddha (beginning) and lives of the beings in the nine worlds (end) are ultimately equal (consistent). Hence, all living beings can become Buddhas once they awaken to the true reality of their own lives, that they themselves are entities of the Mystic Law. Ignorance or awareness of this truth is the only difference between a Buddha and persons of the nine worlds.

The Three Realms of Existence

The final component of three thousand realms is the idea of the three realms of existence. This concept views life from three different standpoints and explains the existence of individual lives in the real world; it elucidates three dimensions in which the Ten Worlds are manifest: the realm of the five components; the realm of living beings; and the realm of the environment. According to this concept, the five components (form, perception, conception, volition, and consciousness); their temporary union, which results in a living being; and the environment in which this being dwells, all manifest one and the same state at the same time.

Realm of the Five Components:
The concept of the **realm of the five components** constitutes an analysis of life's physical and psychic functions, or how life relates to its surroundings. As explained in chapter three, the five components are form, perception, conception, volition and consciousness. Form is the physical aspect of life — the body and the five sensory organs whereby we perceive the outside world. Perception is the function of receiving external information through the sense organs. Conception refers to the function whereby we form ideas about what we have perceived. Volition is the will to initiate action in response to what we

THREE REALMS

A concept that views life from three different standpoints and explains the existence of individual lives in the real world. All three realms manifest the same one of the Ten Worlds at any given time.

+ Realm of the Five Components: An analysis of the nature of a living entity in terms of how it responds to its surroundings.

+ Realm of Living Beings: The individual living being, formed by the temporary union of the five components, who manifests or experiences any of the Ten Worlds. Also the collective body of individuals who interact with one another.

+ Realm of the Environment: The place or land where living beings dwell and carry out life activities.

have perceived and conceived. Finally, consciousness describes the discerning function of life that exercises value judgments, distinguishes good from evil, and so on. It also supports and integrates the other four components.

In terms of life's material and spiritual aspects, we find that form alone corresponds to the physical aspect and the other four components correspond to the spiritual aspect. In line with the Buddhist belief that the spiritual and material aspects of life are essentially one, however, there can be no form without perception, conception, volition and consciousness, and equally there can be no consciousness without form, perception, conception and volition. The same goes for the other three components. The five components, then, should be understood not only individually but as a whole—that is, in terms of their mutual interactions.

This principle explains how life expresses each of the Ten Worlds. For example, someone in the world of Hunger will form a conception of and react to the same object differently than someone in the world of Heaven.

Realm of Living Beings:
In contrast to the realm of the five components, which analyzes living beings in terms of their physical and mental constituents, the **realm of living beings** sees them as integrated individuals who can experience the Ten Worlds. "No man is an island;" each of us lives in a state of continual interrelationship and reciprocal influence. Therefore, the realm of living beings can also be interpreted as the social environment, which includes all the other living beings with whom we interact.

Realm of the Environment:
The **realm of the environment** is easy to understand. All living beings dwell in some sort of environment that supports their existence. This realm therefore includes all insentient life forms, such as mountains, trees, grass and rivers. Moreover, differences in the life-states of living beings are reflected in the land they inhabit — at different times, the land may manifest the states of Anger, Heaven and so on.

While together the Ten Worlds and the ten factors describe aspects shared by all living beings, it is through the concept of the three realms that we can explain why no two beings are ever exactly alike. As we have just seen, the most basic differences expressed in the three realms are those of the Ten Worlds. In addition, there are differences generated from the life of each individual, for the workings of the five components differ from one person to the next, just as karma differs. For example, even among people endowed with the same basic tendency toward

Learning, no two are endowed with exactly the same physical form, and no two will perceive, conceive or react to their environment in exactly the same way. Likewise, no two people have exactly the same social or physical environment. The three realms, then, represent the actual world of the individual.

How the Component Parts Relate

In Nichiren's writings, we find this passage:

> Life at each moment is endowed with the Ten Worlds. At the same time, each of the Ten Worlds is endowed with all Ten Worlds, so that an entity of life actually possesses one hundred worlds. Each of these worlds in turn possesses thirty realms, which means that in the one hundred worlds there are three thousand realms. The three thousand realms of existence are all possessed by life in a single moment. If there is no life, that is the end of the matter. But if there is the slightest bit of life, it contains all the three thousand realms...."[13]

The figure of three thousand was not chosen at random; rather, it reflects the immensity and diversification of life.

Throughout history, people have realized that all natural phenomena are elusive and uncertain, and so they have set out to seek the eternal, unchanging truth of life. Different teachers have explained the relationship between this absolute truth and the ephemeral world we experience. Some have suggested that the ultimate truth governs this world from a higher plane. Others have said that it lies beyond or behind phenomena, or that phenomena are in fact mere illusion and that the ultimate truth alone is real. A similar dualistic tendency is found in some

Buddhist teachings predating the Lotus Sutra, which generally held that the mind is the basis of all phenomena, and that all phenomena arise from the mind. By contrast, the "three thousand realms" principle, based on the Lotus Sutra, has it that the mind (or each moment of our lives) and the phenomena of the universe are "two but not two"—or, essentially, one.

Rather than denoting the objective world outside our lives, however, the "three thousand realms" principle refers to our subjective inner state. This principle doesn't simply stress the importance of frame of mind; it emphasizes the total transformation of one's being, including the environment. The message of the "three thousand realms" principle is that we should seek to establish a firm resolution or deep desire to manifest our greatest potential—to elevate our life-condition to the state of Buddhahood.

This principle demonstrates that every last person has the potential to become a Buddha, awakened to the eternity and boundlessness of life. What people actually experience, however, is different from this potential. Recognizing this difference, T'ien-t'ai formulated two views of three thousand realms—the theoretical and the actual. By "theoretical," he meant the life of common mortals or people influenced by fundamental darkness and in whom the world of Buddhahood remains dormant. In contrast, "actual" meant a life in which Buddhahood is fully active and manifest.

According to the "Expedient Means" chapter of the Lotus Sutra, the eternal Buddha nature is innate in the life of every person, and it is theoretically possible to access this supreme nature. This theory is shown to be an actuality in the sutra's "Life Span of the Thus Come One" chapter, in which Shakyamuni showed how he established his own Buddhahood within and taught through his actual example.

The "Life Span" chapter deals only with Shakyamuni's personal case, however; there is no direct indication that people living today could establish Buddhahood in accord with the "three thousand realms" principle. The Lotus Sutra did affirm theoretically that common mortals are capable of accessing their innate Buddhahood, but no method was overtly revealed.

Nichiren's teachings, therefore, are significant because he identifies a method for actualizing this potential. He wrote: "Nam-myoho-renge-kyo, the heart of the 'Life Span' chapter, is the mother of all Buddhas throughout the ten directions and the three existences."[14] Chanting Nam-myoho-renge-kyo is the practice Nichiren prescribed and through which our Buddhahood is brought forth. Thus, we can manifest the essence of three thousand realms in a single moment of life.

The Oneness of Body and Mind

The "three thousand realms" principle and its component parts give rise to other important principles. Two of the most important are "the oneness of body and mind" and "the oneness of life and environment."

Overall, the ten factors component represents the oneness of the material and the spiritual or oneness of body and mind. In the eighth century, the Chinese Buddhist scholar Miao-lo wrote: "Appearance exists only in what is material; nature exists only in what is spiritual. Entity, power, influence, and relation in principle combine both the material and the spiritual. Internal cause and latent effect are purely spiritual; manifest effect exists only in what is material."[15]

Miao-lo describes appearance as "material" because it represents the physical, outwardly manifest aspect of life. Nature is referred to as "spiritual" because it is identified with the unseen inner aspect; internal cause and latent effect likewise denote things considered spiritual because they are dormant within life. Manifest effect has a perceivable form, and so it is defined as material. Entity, power, influence and relation all entail both material and spiritual aspects of life. And, of course, the other nine factors are integrated by the factor of consistency from beginning to end.

The "oneness of body and mind" is a translation of the Buddhist term *shiki shin funi*, which literally means "body and mind are two but not two" and "body and mind are not two but two." It is one of the ten onenesses, or nondualities, that derive from this understanding of the inseparability of what is spiritual or dormant and what it material or manifest.

Since the early twentieth century, scientists and laypersons alike have become increasingly aware of the need to integrate the various fields of science. Those who attempt this integration are sometimes called "systems scientists." The pioneers of systems science hoped to shed light on the complex interrelations of living organisms not just from an intuitive viewpoint but also from a properly scientific one. To this end, they devised theories and specific methodologies; and they could further demonstrate the applicability of their theories in several areas of knowledge. This approach, emphasizing the reciprocal influences among phenomena, has been applied in many fields including management, sociology, environmental engineering and even mechanical engineering.

Buddhism (and specifically the "three thousand realms" principle) could be considered a "systems science" concerned with understanding the totality of life phenomena. For example, the Buddhist teaching that the mind and body are "two but not two," which is part of a larger philosophical system, is supported by modern scientific research.

Researchers in psychology and physiology have confirmed that there is indeed an interaction between mind and body. For example, emotional stress gives rise to physical symptoms such as ulcers or muscular tension, while physical factors such as vitamin deficiencies or changes in blood-sugar levels can deeply affect a person's emotional state. Even in the nineteenth century, basing his statement on the fact that psychological stress affects the digestive process, Austrian pathologist Karl Rokitansky declared diseases of the stomach to be a direct product of diseases of the brain. Our rapidly increasing understanding of the subtlety of the reciprocal influence of mind and body has contributed to a new science generally called "psychosomatic medicine."

The interrelationship between the material and the spiritual is a pertinent aspect of issues concerning the human brain and the human mind. For instance, there is the ongoing debate as to whether brain death or the cessation of heartbeat should be taken as the legal criterion for a human death.

The brain is often thought of as the locus of the spirit and, as such, is inseparably related to the mind. In his book *Human Options*, Norman Cousins defined the belief system of the individual as not just "a state of mind" but as "a prime physiological reality." Therefore, it is vital that we always choose to do what we believe is correct; otherwise our choice adversely affects the physiological functioning of our brain. Cousins wrote: "Nothing is more wondrous about the fifteen billion neurons in the human brain than their ability to convert thoughts, hopes, ideas, and attitudes into chemical substances."[16]

Even a few neurons in the human brain can, in response to a subtle change in the mind, bring about a series of precise chemical reactions. The power contained within a single brain cell is indeed, to use Cousins's word, wondrous.

The mind–brain relationship is a principal subject of investigation in two fields of science, psychopathology and neurophysiology. Researchers have studied the connection between brain chemistry changes and emotional states such as joy, pleasure, misery and pain. Back in the 1940s and early 1950s, University of Wisconsin psychology professor Harry Harlow explored the change in brain secretions of people recently disappointed in love. Harlow's was only one of many studies that documented how brain secretions increase or diminish in response to thoughts, behavior, environment and other factors.

Even the closest scrutiny of our brain cells, however, fails to reveal the nature of the spirit. Spiritual activity may be impossible without brain cells; nevertheless, the brain is only the physical seat of such activity. The Canadian neurosurgeon Wilder Penfield conducted extensive experiments during the 1930s and 1940s to determine whether the mind is located in the brain. He devised a surgical technique to treat patients suffering from focal epilepsy, during which he studied individuals' reactions to electrical stimulation of various parts of the brain. He discovered, for example, that when the visual or auditory areas were stimulated, the patient would hallucinate. Likewise, if a motor area was stimulated, a person might involuntarily move a limb. Through discovering that electrical stimulation of corresponding brain areas could cause people to see, hear, smell, etc., Penfield contributed greatly to understanding how the information the brain receives through the sense organs is processed.

Most interesting about his experiments is that Penfield's patients reported their surprise at responding consciously to the stimuli—they had not responded voluntarily; rather it felt as though they were following the dictates of some outside force. Penfield determined that while the brain may be the body's computer, the mind is its programmer.

He further concluded that the mind's highly evolved and sophisticated functions (such as belief, decision-making and value judgment) cannot be activated solely by electrical stimulation as he used in his experiments. In Penfield's view, the brain is the physical vehicle of the psyche; or, more precisely, the physical locus of mental activity.

Penfield also researched how memories are stored in the brain, focusing on the temporal lobe, an area smaller than a human palm found just beneath the region of the temple and the ear. Penfield reported that when this area was electrically stimulated, patients seemed to vividly relive scenes from the past along with accompanying thoughts and sensations. What's more, they remembered things long gone from their memories. One man, for example, recollected his childhood acquaintances, other children with whom he had fought and a thief who had broken into his house. In light of Penfield's experiments, perhaps the memories of everything we have experienced are somehow stored in our brain.

Dr. Yasunori Chiba, a Japanese neurophysiologist, has estimated that the amount of data—in computer jargon, the number of bits—an individual can commit to memory over seventy years, both consciously and unconsciously, is approximately fifteen trillion. One Buddhist sutra explains that in a single day some 804,000 thoughts cross an individual's mind; multiplied by seventy years the total is approximately twenty-one trillion. The sutra's precise figure of 804,000 should not be taken literally, however—it simply means a large number. Nevertheless, Chiba's figure suggests that science may one day prove that each individual has access to memories extending back to the origin of the human species and beyond.

No one knows exactly where our memories are stored in the brain. Yet they emerge in response to stimuli from or in association with the external world. Neurophysiologic studies have shown that the hypothalamus and the limbic system are associated with primal responses such as anger and fear, yet such emotions do not arise unless relevant parts of the brain are stimulated. We might say they are latent within the human body.

We know that the two cerebral hemispheres have different functions. The left hemisphere is associated with logic, calculation and language, while the right hemisphere is more concerned with sensitivity, intuition and imagination. A "bridge" called the corpus callosum, which contains some 200 million nerve fibers, joins the two hemispheres. Roger Sperry, a professor of psychobiology and 1981 winner of the Nobel Prize in physiology or medicine, developed experimental techniques whereby information could be fed into one or the other cerebral hemispheres of a so-called "split-brain" patient—whose corpus callosum has been severed—so that the responses of the two hemispheres could be observed independently. Sperry's work demonstrated that a conscious mind exists in each hemisphere.

The Buddhist concept of the oneness of body and mind accords with the discoveries of science, particularly those demonstrating the profound interrelationship between our physical bodies and material world and what we regard as the spiritual, or life's intangible aspects. Buddhism recognizes the physical and the spiritual—two separate classes of phenomena —as indivisible and continuous because they are both aspects of the same ultimate reality. When we distinguish between the material and the spiritual, we are operating on the level of phenomena; when we talk of their oneness, we are talking in terms of the ultimate reality. "The oneness of body and mind" therefore describes the ultimate reality of life.

Life and Its Environment

The principle of the oneness of life and its environment similarly derives from the ten factors and the three realms. As previously explained, Buddhism teaches that a living being is formed from the temporary union of the five components. This union constitutes a subjective self that experiences the karmic consequences of its past actions. But there must also be a domain in which karmic consequences find expression. This domain is the last of the three realms: the realm of the environment. In contrast, the five components and living beings—the first two of the three realms—correspond to life.

Both life and its environment exhibit the manifest effect produced by the factors of internal cause, relation and latent effect. Because self and environment are two integral aspects of any individual, the effects of karma appear both in us and in our environment. The word *environment* here does not mean the overall context in which all beings live. Rather, it refers to the fact that each living being has its own unique environment in which the effects of its individual karma appear. In this sense, the formation of one's environment coincides with that person's birth into this world. Life and its environment are often viewed as being totally distinct, but on the most fundamental level they are one and inseparable.

Perhaps many places in the universe can serve as fitting environments for life. The earth remains hospitable to life because of an extremely subtle environmental balance. With the enormous power we have acquired through technological advances, we are now having an influence on this delicate balance. As the science of ecology becomes more sophisticated, scientists' concern that people work more actively to preserve the biosphere grows stronger.

About ten thousand years ago, what is now the Sahara Desert was blanketed in lush grass. It seems to have been a cultural center because a vast variety of ancient artifacts have been found scattered across it. During the time of the Roman Empire, part of the Sahara even seems to have served as a granary. It is generally accepted that the Sahara became a desert as a result of climatic changes and excessive grazing.

Today, such phenomena as droughts and floods seem to occur with even greater frequency than they did in the past. And added to these natural catastrophes are human-made ones, which are the inevitable consequence of modern civilization's view that human beings and nature are two irreconcilably different entities.

Through the latter part of the nineteenth century, Western science was largely based on mechanistic ideas—the universe was, in effect, a giant clock, and all phenomena could be explained in terms of clockwork. Since the early twentieth century, however, attempts to integrate the findings of diverse specialized fields and to understand life in its totality have grown in both number and frequency.

Life can be understood only through a viewpoint that integrates all of its activities. Nichiren Buddhism fosters exactly this holistic view, one that encompasses not just the individual but the entire cosmos and is well suited to the age.

Nichiren wrote: "The ten directions are the 'environment,' and living beings are 'life.' To illustrate, environment is like the shadow, and life, the body. Without the body, no shadow can exist, and without life, no environment. In the same way, life is shaped by its environment."[17] "Ten directions" indicates the entire dimension of space, represented by the eight major points of the compass plus the zenith and the nadir. The subjective self, or life, and the objective world, or environment, share a symbiotic relationship.

The oneness of life and its environment further suggests that individuals can influence and reform their environments through inner change or through the elevation of their basic life-state. Just as any living being contains the potential to dwell in any of the Ten Worlds, so does its environment; and whatever state we bring forth in our lives will be simultaneously manifested in our surroundings. If our basic tendency is toward Hell, we will draw anguish and misery out of our surroundings, but if our basic state is Bodhisattva or Buddhahood, we will enjoy the protection and support of the world around us. By elevating our basic state, then, we can transform our external reality.

It is a common human failing to blame our sufferings on things outside ourselves — other people, circumstances beyond our control and so on — rather than to look for the causes within us. If we base our lives on the principle that life and its environment are one, however, we see that the fundamental cause of all our trials and tribulations lies not in the environment but in ourselves.

Nichiren wrote: "If the minds of living beings are impure, their land is also impure, but if their minds are pure, so is their land. There are not two lands, pure or impure in themselves. The difference lies solely in the good or evil of our minds."[18] This passage tells us that there is a practical method for reforming our world — a reformation of ourselves.

As Nichiren explained, life is shaped by its environment. Aspects of the broader environment's influence on human beings are studied in such sciences as bioclimatology, biometeorology and meteorological medicine. Less scientifically, folk wisdom holds that a long period of cloudy weather may cause people to feel gloomy, or that the impending arrival of low atmospheric pressure will cause old wounds to ache. In fact, such claims seem to have a genuine physiological basis. Most of us recognize the subtle physiological changes brought about by atmospheric conditions. Perhaps this is why doctors sometimes prescribe "a change of air." Immersing oneself in nature is not only spiritually refreshing, it also clears the head, because trees emit minute traces of substances called phytoncides, the inhalation of which enhances our nervous system and sharpens our thought process.

Harvey Cushing, the great American neurosurgeon of the late nineteenth and early twentieth century, said: "A physician is obligated to consider more than a diseased organ, more even than the whole man—he must view the man in his world."[19] What he was suggesting, and what Buddhism suggests, is that our health depends, in a sense, on how we adapt to the challenges presented to us by our surroundings.

Even within our own bodies, the oneness of life and its environment is evident. If we look at ourselves as a single entity, our lives at each moment correspond to "life" and the workings of our bodies' cells and molecules to our "environment." In our every activity the two are inseparable. The cells and molecules (the environment that supports us) go on about their vital business as expressions of the three thousand realms at work in our lives at each moment.

The very state of aliveness may be understood as a continuing relationship between life's generating power and the body's various components. Nearly sixty trillion cells work independently yet together to function as a human being. But the human body is far more than just a collection of cells and organs. The various cells, organs and bodily systems maintain a creative balance between specialization and synthesis. They each display their individual character while coordinating their activities into a harmonious unity.

Social psychologist Kurt Lewin coined the term *life space*, by which he meant the individual's psychological environment as he or she perceives it. Lewin's perspective bears many similarities to the concept of the oneness of life and its environment. He emphasized the internal over the external environment of living beings. Accordingly, he saw the environment as not just the objective world but also as an important component of the living beings dwelling in that world. Lewin claimed that all life forms on this planet have their own environment, meaning that there are as many environments as there are living beings. Even the cat or dog we keep as a pet has its own environment, in Lewin's view. In the course of creating their unique environments, living beings participate in a play of mutual influence with other living beings and with external phenomena.

Advances in medical technology have given us devices capable of exploring almost every aspect of a person's anatomy; computed tomography and magnetic resonance imaging are two examples. Before CT and MRI techniques were developed, bones often obscured X-rays. But today every part of the body can be examined in remarkable detail. MRI devices produce what amounts to an atomic-level examination of the oneness of life and its environment—of the various atoms that constitute the human body, some nuclei (such as that of the hydrogen atom) resonate in a strong magnetic field, giving rise to a characteristic energy profile. The resulting signals are processed through a computer to produce an image of the body's interior. To the naked eye, there is an obvious distinction between the inner human body and the external world, but in the submicroscopic world of the atom there is no such obvious demarcation; both are composed of the same elements and atoms.

Another example of the oneness of life and its environment is the level of salt in our bodily fluids. The level is apparently close to that of seawater. Some evolutionary scientists say this is because the life forms from which we are descended evolved in the ocean. Toward the end of the nineteenth century, the British physiologist Sydney Ringer attempted to create a laboratory solution of salts that would prolong the life of excised animal tissues immersed in it. He produced various combinations of organic salts but was unsuccessful. After much work, he discovered that a frog's heart had kept on beating in one of his solutions. One of his assistants, it turned out, had accidentally used tap water in preparing the solution, thereby introducing calcium and other inorganic substances. Thanks to this error, he established the correct composition for his Ringer's Solution, which is still in use today.

Our bodies are composed of various elements common throughout the universe—hydrogen, oxygen, carbon. If you weigh 154 pounds, you are made up of roughly 97 pounds of oxygen, 29 pounds of carbon, 14 pounds of hydrogen, and 8 pounds of nitrogen; the other 6 pounds consist of potassium, calcium, phosphorus, sulfur and other trace elements (including gold, which would account for about .0002 of an ounce).

Nichiren wrote: "All phenomena are contained within one's life, down to the last particle of dust. The nine mountains and the eight seas are encompassed in one's body...."[20] Here he was referring to the mountains and seas that, according to ancient Indian cosmology, constitute the world. In another writing, he stated, "one's body imitates in detail the heaven and the Earth."[21] This implies that not only are our bodies fundamentally the same as our physical world but our lives and life force itself are indivisible. The Mystic Law—Nam-myoho-renge-kyo—which "summarizes" life force, expresses itself simultaneously as living beings and as the environments in which they live. The two are one, united in that they both are manifestations of the fundamental law of life.

"Survival of the fittest" is regarded, simplistically, as the dominant factor in evolution. According to this idea, through random mutations certain organisms adapt better to their environment than others and so are more likely to survive and reproduce, passing on their improved characteristics to their offspring. But scientists in fields ranging from ecology to molecular biology have cast doubt on this process. One pioneer of a "new evolution," the Japanese scientist Kinji Imanishi, says that living beings play a dominant role in their own evolution. And he suggests they not only select the location of their habitat but also actually transform themselves in response to changing circumstances in that particular locale. His theory proposes that the driving force of evolution consists not of random physical mutations but of living beings' ability to make choices. It also emphasizes the inseparable relationship between evolution and the environment. In this respect, certainly, Imanishi's ideas come close to the Buddhist view of life.

According to scientific theory, the earth was formed about 4.6 billion years ago. During the following one or two billion years, the planet's ability to support life increased slowly until the most primitive life forms developed. Exactly how they did so is still something of a mystery, but it is likely that volcanism on an unimaginable scale, the "organic soup" of the oceans, and myriad chemical reactions in the atmosphere all played their part. If we view life as an essential force inherent in the universe, we can assume that our planet from the outset had a tendency toward the emergence of life. This tendency made primitive life possible while simultaneously bringing about the preconditions for its appearance.

According to this view, all life forms, including us, were born from an insentient realm, the environment of the universe. T'ien-t'ai called the place from which life emerges "the ultimate depth of life, that being the absolute reality."[22] In these ideas, we find the great significance of the oneness of life and its environment. Nichiren defined T'ien-t'ai's "ultimate depth of life" as the most fundamental law of life and the universe—Nam-myoho-renge-kyo—which is itself the cosmic life force; it is the Buddha nature inherent in all things, whether sentient or insentient, throughout the universe.

Looking Ahead

Each individual life contains all the various laws of the universe as well as the fundamental power that underlies all phenomena. Each moment of our individual lives is exactly equivalent to the cosmic life. Far too often, though, we fixate on the idea that we are separate beings, failing to realize that all life is indivisible.

Nichiren defined true independence as our awakening to and maintaining harmony with the ultimate Law of life. Establishing this independence is synonymous with revealing the Buddha nature within our lives; it is the ability to use our individual given circumstances as a means for growth, rather than being restricted or controlled by illusions and the sufferings of life and death. In light of the concept of the mutual possession of the Ten Worlds, we should try to establish the state of Buddhahood as the basis of everything we do.

When our inherent Buddhahood comes to the fore, our innate power (one of the ten factors) of universal compassion and wisdom moves into action. Through the law of cause and effect (also included among the ten factors) the manifestation of Buddhahood is further strengthened so that it becomes integral to all our experience.

As our Buddha nature emerges, so do the four qualities of

Buddhahood, or four virtues—eternity, happiness, true self and purity. The virtue of *eternity* is the boundless freedom of one awakened to the eternity of life. *Happiness* is an inner joy and fulfillment that cannot be destroyed by any outside influence. *True self* means the establishment of a genuine independence that is absolute and indestructible. Finally, *purity* is a life free from illusions and sufferings, which a person can maintain even while living and working in an impure society.

If we possess these qualities, our existence will be joyful, happy, pure and secure despite whatever difficulties we may face. Our voyage through the stormy seas of life and death will be directed toward the highest of objectives—the revelation of the Buddhahood of all beings.

When we establish Buddhahood as our basic state, we can then properly harmonize the other nine worlds and thereby make positive use of the time spent dwelling in them; moreover, we can give full play to the five components so that we can fully develop our individual qualities. We can build lasting happiness, invulnerable to any changes in our surroundings. And, with universal compassion, we can have a good influence on everyone we encounter, thereby transforming our environment.

This idea of Buddhahood—the fundamental truth of life—is further clarified by the concept of the nine consciousnesses, which we will explore in the next chapter.

CHAPTER SIX

The Nine Consciousnesses

B UDDHISM EXPLAINS that erroneous perception, conception or consciousness is the cause of suffering. The first step, for example, along the eightfold path is right view—to perceive things as they really are. Therefore, Buddhism reveals that true enlightenment—replacing delusions that distort reality with the wisdom to perceive the true reality—is the way to emancipate ourselves from suffering. These ideas are the basis of the nine consciousnesses concept.

Many attempts have been made in the West to explore the different levels of human consciousness, most notably through psychoanalysis and depth psychology. Neurology and neurophysiology, too, have sought objectively to examine such functions as sensation, emotion, understanding and memory in connection with the workings of the brain. Buddhism, by contrast, examines the depths of our lives more intuitively. Yet a Buddhist concept such as the nine consciousnesses yields much insight into the same areas of the human condition addressed by major hypotheses of modern science and medicine.

In Buddhism, *consciousness* is the translation of the Sanskrit *vijnana*, which means ability of discernment, comprehension or perception. Shakyamuni included the function of *vijnana* among the five components—form, perception, conception, volition and consciousness. Consciousness is usually understood as conscious awareness, the ability to think or a common waking state. In this chapter, however, the word *consciousness* is used to mean something different. In Buddhism, consciousness implies a capacity or energy that operates whether or not we are consciously aware of it.

Consciousness operates on several levels. The nine consciousnesses concept, developed largely in the T'ien-t'ai and Flower Garland schools of sixth-century China, analyzes the various strata of consciousness and thereby clarifies the operations of life itself. This concept is different from the idea of the Ten Worlds. In T'ien-t'ai's teaching, however, these two Buddhist theories overlap in that the ninth consciousness can be understood as synonymous with the tenth world — Buddhahood. Nichiren did not expound the nine consciousnesses concept, but he adopted its bottom line that the ninth consciousness is equal to Buddhahood.

Each living being assimilates information from its surroundings and adjusts itself accordingly. Beings depend for their survival on the ability to perceive and respond to their environment. Even plants can sense the change of seasons and adjust to the differences in winter and summer weather. In winter, for instance, deciduous trees shed their large leaves so as not to lose too much moisture through them.

Likewise, human beings have the ability to respond to their environment. For example, we can discern what is and isn't edible. Just looking at fruit in a bowl, we can usually tell if it is made of wax. But even if our senses of smell and touch were deceived, we could try tasting a piece and quickly find out if it were imitation. Discernment or perception is necessary for living beings to survive.

The First Six Consciousnesses:
Sensory Perception and Integration

The first five of the nine consciousnesses correspond to the conventional notion of the five senses: sight, hearing, smell, taste and touch. They are activated whenever our five sensory organs —eyes, ears, nose, tongue and skin—interact with our environment. The five sense organs are like windows, or perhaps pathways, by which the external world is connected to the internal, and they function in a relatively passive manner.

The sixth consciousness integrates the perceptions of the five senses into coherent mental images and makes judgments about the external world. If any of the five sensory organs are not functioning well, the mind likewise can be limited in its ability to accurately perceive the outer world. Conversely, even if a "window" is clouded, one's mind still can make sound judgments if the other senses function well. The sixth consciousness can also function independently of the five senses as in dreams or uses of the imagination.

More often than not, the function of the five senses is distorted. Negative influences arising from the sixth, seventh and eighth consciousnesses, as we shall see, distort the mind's perception of the outer world. Our perceptions are influenced by our attitudes, by the effects of our karma and by the inner workings of consciousness. To a healthy person filled with vitality, even simple food will taste delicious, while for one plunged in grief, even the most sumptuous feast will taste bland. Phenomena such as these are mysterious yet commonplace.

Also, each sense organ possesses a consciousness of its own. Physiologically speaking, the sense organs do not pass on to the brain everything that they perceive. Rather, they select and transmit only the "important" things. So when we talk about the consciousness of the eyes, for example, we are referring to the eyes' own power to discern or select. Say we are desperately looking for our keys. As usual in such situations, they are right in the center of the living room, but still we do not see them. We may search frantically, yet the keys remain lost because our eyes have "selected" what information will be sent to our brain —we have pre-supposed that the keys could not possibly be in the middle of the living room. (After all, we would have *seen* them if they were there!) Because of our fixed belief, the information picked up by our eyes—that the keys are in the living room—is not relayed to our brain.

Buddhist practice is said to "purify" the senses and the other levels of consciousness so that we can perceive all phenomena clearly and accurately. Again, the sense organs are the interface between the small universe of our lives and the cosmos. To purify our sense organs, then, means to completely harmonize our lives with the universe, "tuning in" to its rhythm. One who has purified the sense of sight will find even the most mundane scene to be a miracle sparkling with life. And one who has purified the sense of hearing can hear Mozart in the cacophony of a baby's cries.

A passage from the Lotus Sutra reads: "If good men or good women accept and uphold this Lotus Sutra, if they read it, recite it, explain and preach it, or transcribe it, such persons will obtain eight hundred eye benefits, twelve hundred ear benefits, eight hundred nose benefits, twelve hundred tongue benefits, eight hundred body benefits, and twelve hundred mind benefits. With these benefits they will be able to adorn their six sense organs, making all of them pure."[1]

This passage mentions various kinds of practice, what Buddhism terms "the five practices": accepting and upholding the Lotus Sutra, reading it, reciting it, explaining or preaching it, and transcribing it. In Nichiren Buddhism, the one practice of accepting and upholding the law of Nam-myoho-renge-kyo includes the five practices in their entirety. The first six consciousnesses are purified as we embrace Nam-myoho-renge-kyo and strive to break through our limitations, transforming suffering into joy.

The deaf and blind can purify their senses as well. Lacking certain senses does not preclude people from perceiving the essence of all things any more than having perfect vision or hearing automatically endows them with such perception. Regardless of our physical limitations, we can, through Buddhist practice, fully develop the sense of the heart. Purifying the senses refers, in part, to gaining insight into the nature of all phenomena.

As a result of scientific advances, our eyes and ears have become vastly more powerful; we can see into outer space and hear sounds from the depths of the sea. But does such power equal happiness? While science tends to direct its investigations ever outward, it will only produce misfortune if there is no corresponding growth and maturation in the inner realm of life.

What's more, science has yet to invent an instrument that gives us insight into someone's heart. Buddhism enables us to perceive our own hearts and the hearts of others, to thoroughly understand how the heart operates. We might say Buddhism is the science of the spirit, the medicine of the heart. Ultimately, purifying the heart—our perceptions and intentions—is the foundation for purifying our sense organs and our consciousness.

To Helen Keller, who triumphed over her inability to speak, hear or see, Mark Twain said, "Helen, the world is full of unseeing eyes, vacant, staring, soulless eyes."[2] Twain also remarked that the two most interesting characters of the nineteenth century were Napoleon and Helen Keller, noting that while

Napoleon had planned to conquer the world by means of force and failed, Helen Keller, while bearing the weight of a threefold disability, succeeded through her abundant spiritual strength.[3]

The Seventh Consciousness: Ego or Lesser Self

The first six consciousnesses are responses to the everyday external world of phenomena. These functions are easily recognizable as they operate on the "outer surface" of the mind—that is, in our conscious realm. Aside from exceptions such as dreaming, in which the sixth consciousness operates on its own, the first six consciousnesses perpetually respond to constant input from our surroundings. Because they function continuously from one moment to the next, it is easy to assume that we possess an unchanging self and that perhaps this self oversees and controls the six consciousnesses.

The function that leads us to believe in the existence of a permanent self is called the seventh consciousness. This seventh level represents the internal, spiritual world and is the source of identity of the self, operating in the name of self-preservation and expansion. It seems to correspond to the Western idea of the ego.

In reality, the self is in constant flux, changing moment to moment, as do our bodies and all other phenomena. Because instinctively we are "attached" to the self or ego, we sense it as somehow constant. We remember events in our lives and construct a narrative about who we are. Without that capacity, it would be difficult to function in the world. Attachment to this fleeting self becomes problematic, however, when we mistake it for a changeless entity and therefore stop seeking what is *truly* changeless and profound.

The seventh consciousness is also characterized by the ability to distinguish oneself from others, to establish a boundary between self and other. And it is the source of the drive to preserve oneself. Again, it would be difficult for us to function in the real world if we did not have this capacity.

Ultimately, however, this drive or desire creates suffering. We can be deeply controlled by the function of the seventh consciousness and the notion of self it produces, believing it to be substantial when, in reality, it is not. Attachment to this self can breed arrogance and egotism as well as self-loathing and insecurity. Yet, if we abandon this self we are apt to fear that we are negating our existence. So we cling to the stories we tell ourselves about who we are; and we seek to expand these stories, reinforcing our opinions and beliefs, our likes and dislikes, etc., as if protecting the core of our identity. We thus lose sight of the true self, which lies at a deeper level of consciousness, and remain ignorant of our true potential. Our attachment to the self of the seventh consciousness confines us in a small cage within the vastness of life, and our inherent wellspring of humanity remains untapped.

While it may seem the word *self* is being employed negatively, implying selfish or self-seeking behavior, this usage is what Buddhism regards as the "lesser self." As discussed in previous chapters, there is also a "greater self," the true self lying dormant in the depths of life. The whole of Buddhist philosophy centers on the idea of breaking out of the prison of the lesser self to reveal the infinitely expanded true self. The nine consciousnesses concept was developed to achieve this goal.

Thus, while the beneficent potential of the seventh consciousness is undeniable, its potential for creating the "cages" of ego must not be overlooked.

The Eighth Consciousness: Karmic Storehouse

All experiences from our present and previous lifetimes accumulate in the eighth consciousness, believed to be the realm that undergoes the cycle of birth and death. The eighth is also known as the *alaya*-consciousness—the Sanskrit word *alaya* meaning "repository" or "storehouse." This consciousness receives the results of thoughts, words and deeds and stores them as karmic potentials or "seeds." Since karmic seeds are found only at a very deep level of life, they are unaffected by the external world. Nevertheless, there is a reciprocal influence between the seeds lying deep in the *alaya*-consciousness and the surface levels of consciousness, where the three kinds of action —thinking, speaking and doing—are carried out.

On the most practical level, the seeds stored in the *alaya*-consciousness influence the workings of our first seven consciousnesses. Karma affects every aspect of body and mind. People recognize and respond to the same circumstances in different ways, depending on their personalities. Certain physical attributes, too, such as body shape, may reflect lifestyle, eating habits, biological makeup and environment. Spiritual condition reflects lifestyle as well as experience and knowledge. Thus, through the workings of our karma, we have arrived physically and spiritually at our current state of life. The reward or retribution of karma primarily expresses itself in the form of one's internal state of life. It will also be reflected externally in an individual's environment or social sphere.

According to Josei Toda: "All of our actions in past existences are contained in their entirety in our lives…. While we might want to say, 'What I did in the past is irrelevant; I was born with a clean slate,' we cannot escape our past so easily. 'Why was I born poor?' 'Why was I born stupid?' 'Why is my business failing

even though I am working as hard as I can?' The answer to all of
these questions is to be found in our past lives."[4]

According to medical science, over several years, every cell in
our bodies, from the center of our eyeballs to the marrow of our
bones, is replaced, Toda continued. On that basis, he said, you
could argue that you are not liable for a debt from five years ago
—in a sense, it was a physically different "you" who incurred the
debt. Still, the debt collector will come without fail. Similarly,
we have no choice but to take responsibility for our past actions
and the karma we've created.

No matter what our circumstances now, however, we can
freely improve ourselves through the actions we take from this
point on. To be superficially content with the way we are, or to
chide ourselves for our circumstances, ultimately creates no
value. Buddhism teaches us to move toward creating value,
toward cultivating deeper wisdom and compassion. We may
make mistakes in the course of our lives, but if we reflect upon
our past attitude and behavior, we can use our sorrows and
mishaps as a springboard for development.

The *Alaya*-Consciousness and Death

At the time of death, one's life moves into a latent state—from
sentience to insentience—in three stages. First, the operations
of the first five consciousnesses become latent, while the sixth
consciousness continues to function. Second, the sixth consciousness recedes into dormancy, becoming latent within the
eighth, or *alaya*-consciousness, while the seventh consciousness
remains active as a passionate attachment to temporary existence. Third, the seventh consciousness, too, lapses into latency
within the *alaya*-consciousness. Hence, it is only the eighth and
ninth levels of consciousness that constitute the "vessel" of

eternal life — continuing throughout the endless cycle of life and death.

During the transition from sentience to insentience, our capacity to respond to external stimuli becomes latent and our lives become fixed in whichever state we have established as our basic tendency. So, as death approaches, less and less can we use worldly means to alter our basic life-condition. Wealth, power, social standing, the love of others — none of these can help us, and even great thoughts and philosophies, if we have understood them only superficially without making them a part of our lives, will prove utterly useless in the face of imminent death. As life shifts into a latent state, our power to influence the environment and to be influenced by it is lost.

The *alaya*-consciousness is sometimes called "nonvanishing" because the karmic seeds stored within it do not disappear at death. Our individual lives are accompanied into latency by all the effects of our karma. Although habits, talents, abilities, traits and the like will not carry over, the elements that will determine our life-condition after death remain within the *alaya*-consciousness. For example, the *alaya*-consciousness of someone who has established the tendency of Hell will in death go through hellish sufferings resulting from causes made while alive. A person continually governed by desire will be tormented by frustration all the more after death.

Our karmic energy mutually impacts our loved ones (living and deceased) and indeed all humankind. It even affects animals and plants. A positive change in the karmic energy in the depths of one's life becomes a cogwheel for change in the lives of others; one person's internal reformation — or "human revolution" — therefore, can change the destiny of that person's family and society.

It is important to remember that while alive, the self changes moment to moment; we continually make new causes through physical and spiritual actions. The effects of past causes are revealed through this process, in turn triggering more changes and giving us more opportunities to create new karmic causes. Even though we can create new karmic seeds, however, the *alaya*-consciousness can never be entirely free from delusion. Complete purity is to be found only in the ninth consciousness.

The Ninth Consciousness: Purity, Greater Self, Buddha Nature

Not only our thoughts but also our words and deeds are registered deep in our lives. Our karma combines both good and bad, or enlightenment and delusion—opposing forces locked in a never-ending struggle. Based on compassion, we can arouse a determination to make causes that offset the karmic effects imprinted on the *alaya*-consciousness through delusion. We can work toward self-reformation by breaking through the walls of egoism and dedicating our lives to the benefit of others. In this way, we can significantly affect the *alaya*-consciousness.

Theoretically, to overcome the negative influences of past deeds, we would have to spend as long a time making good causes as we spent accumulating bad ones since the infinite past—replacing each bad seed in the storehouse with a good one by one. And we would carefully have to avoid adding new bad causes! Changing our destiny would seem almost impossible, then, since we live in what some Buddhist scriptures call a "defiled age" in which we cannot help creating new bad karmic causes. But this bleak outlook stems from a cause-and-effect theory grounded in only the first eight consciousnesses.

The nine consciousnesses concept explains that we can radically break through our accumulated bad karma. Nichiren teaches that even people of little virtue or who have committed great offenses, will, by accessing the deeper currents of life, receive the same effects as if they had made many good causes in the past. How does this work?

The ninth or *amala*-consciousness is the key to transforming the dynamics of the *alaya*-consciousness. The Sanskrit word *amala* means "pure," "stainless" or "spotless." As its name suggests, the *amala*-consciousness remains eternally untainted by karmic accretions. The karmic storehouse, with its accumulation of bad karmic seeds, has become fouled with the three poisons, like the gases arising from a trash dump. A pure clean stream gushes forth from the depths of our lives once the ninth level of consciousness is opened, and all impurities simultaneously and immediately are swept away like detritus washed from the street in a spring shower.

The ninth consciousness is itself the ultimate reality of all things and is equivalent to the universal Buddha nature. Buddhism teaches that we can change our deepest karma through drawing upon this inner capacity of our lives rather than through the intervention of an external god.

The *amala*-consciousness is pure life force, the power to live, and it represents the drive to have a better life. It is the greater self that works for the happiness of all. The power to make all people absolutely happy is the function of the Buddha. Therefore, the ninth consciousness is known as the Buddha consciousness. It is also called the Dharma nature, which denotes the enlightenment potential in every being. The pure *amala*-consciousness allows us to transform the entire interlocking web of latent causes and effects that forms the *alaya*-consciousness so that it is based on Buddha wisdom rather than delusion.

Tapping the *amala*-consciousness impacts all the other consciousnesses, causing them to express the immense power and infinite wisdom of the Buddha nature. From the standpoint of the *amala*-consciousness, we can see that our karmic accumulations are in essence opportunities to manifest our Buddhahood. Our seventh consciousness—in which we distinguish self from other—becomes the "seat of perception" in which we view everything equally as precious and respectable. In other words, we can surmount our small ego and recognize the equality of all. The sixth consciousness will drop its erroneous preconceptions and see the individual value of all things. The five senses or consciousnesses will contribute to accomplishing the work of the Buddha.

The nine consciousnesses concept, analyzing as it does the various layers of an individual's life and simultaneously shedding light on that life's totality, offers insights for the fields of medicine and psychiatry. In recent decades, psychosomatic medicine therapies have included Buddhist-related ideas. For example, in helping people overcome resentment and ill will, doctors may employ a therapy somewhat akin to Buddhist compassion. They instruct the patient to form a clear mental image of the person who is the object of resentment. The patient is then told to picture good things happening to the other person, imagining that person receiving love, attention, money or whatever the patient feels the hate-object would most like.

Similarly, Shakyamuni taught a form of meditation in which one first generates compassionate thoughts toward his or her loved ones and then extends these to people he or she actively dislikes. In this way, one can learn to master anger, a major source of delusion and harmful desires.

Tapping our inner wisdom, compassion and life force is crucial. The full value of the nine consciousnesses concept is demonstrated only when one practically brings forth the ninth consciousness, or Buddhahood.

Nichiren gave concrete expression to the *amala*-consciousness—the fundamental reality of life—in Nam-myoho-renge-kyo. He thereby opened a path through which all people can reveal Buddhahood, drawing forth their latent greater self. "The body is the palace of the ninth consciousness, the unchanging reality,"[5] he wrote, and concluded that chanting Nam-myoho-renge-kyo is the way to open the Buddhahood inherent in our lives, allowing it to gush forth and purify our lives from the inside out.

Nichiren also wrote: "You should base your mind on the ninth consciousness, and carry out your practice in the six consciousnesses."[6] By establishing faith in the ultimate reality and incorporating Buddhist practice into our daily lives, we can access infinite wisdom, power and compassion; we can achieve a fundamental inner reformation and establish an unshakable foundation for true happiness. By analogy, while a piece of wood floating in a stream will be swept away at the whim of the current, even the most powerful of currents cannot shift an island of rock.

Josei Toda used to emphasize that having a life-state of Buddhahood, or absolute happiness, means having the capacity to experience joy under any circumstances. He would say: "When you achieve absolute happiness, you have no money troubles, and you enjoy good health. Your home is peaceful, your business goes well, your heart is filled with a sense of abundance, and everything you see or hear makes you think, 'How delightful!' When the world appears to you in this way, then this world...becomes a Buddha land. That is attaining Buddhahood."[7] He would say that even a quarrel with your spouse, for example, can be joyful. And that when you get angry, you do so with contentment.

Happiness is not reliant solely on the environment. There

are people living in mansions who spend their days in tears. Neither, however, is our happiness entirely independent of our environment. Who, for example, could honestly claim to be happy if they could not feed their children? A person controlled by a negative environment is suffering, whereas one who can control and influence a difficult situation is quite the opposite. We can say, then, that a person with strong life force is happy.

Looking Ahead

The nine consciousnesses philosophy clarifies the distinction between wisdom and delusion, which are both functions of life. The first eight consciousnesses are looked upon as delusion, while the ninth consciousness is viewed as the domain of wisdom. The nine consciousnesses teaching opens an avenue for changing delusion (consciousness) into wisdom (the ninth consciousness).

The nine consciousnesses concept illustrates the complexity of human consciousness as well as the necessity of opening the ninth consciousness, or Buddhahood— the pure life force that cleanses all consciousness of delusion, enabling us to become absolutely happy.

If our life force is weak and frail, even minor problems can overwhelm us, making us miserable. By enhancing our life force even a bit, we gain the vitality to resolve problems—within the home, for example. Stepping out into the community, however, we may find ourselves stymied by problems there. Or say we develop sufficient life force to address issues involving the peace and prosperity of the nation; we still have to face the frequent bewilderments and sufferings of birth, aging, sickness and death.

The Lotus Sutra, the essence of which is crystallized in the phrase *Nam-myoho-renge-kyo*, enables us to tap the life force of the universe so that, no matter what happens, we are never bound by our difficulties.

Enhancing our life force and revealing our Buddha nature are the natural and absolute results of practicing the teachings of Nichiren Buddhism. The next and final chapter delves into the Mystic Law — Nam-myoho-renge-kyo — itself, as well as the Gohonzon, the means devised by Nichiren for connecting the individual with the universal potential for enlightenment.

CHAPTER SEVEN

Nam-myoho-renge-kyo

NICHIREN ESTABLISHED a simple yet profound way of Buddhist practice that enables all human beings to reveal the ultimate truth of their own lives. If we are to manifest our Buddhahood, Nichiren taught, our primary practice must be to chant Nam-myoho-renge-kyo.

Nichiren wrote: "Practicing only the seven characters of Nam-myoho-renge-kyo seems limited, but since they are the master of all the Buddhas of the three existences, the teacher of all the bodhisattvas in the ten directions, and the guide that enables all living beings to attain the Buddha way, it is profound."[1]

The Essence of the Sutra Is Found in Its Title

Nam-myoho-renge-kyo is sometimes referred to as the *daimoku* (title) of the Lotus Sutra. In Sanskrit, the title of the Lotus Sutra is *Saddharma-pundarika-sutra*, meaning literally, "The Sutra of the Lotus Blossom of the Wonderful Law."

Legend has it that there were six Chinese translations of the Lotus Sutra. In 406, the great scholar Kumarajiva, of Kucha in Central Asia, translated the best-known and by far the most popular version. His superb translation became the definitive one and helped win the Lotus Sutra wide respect. Its Chinese title, *Miao-fa-lien-hua-ching,* renders in Japanese as Myoho-renge-kyo.

Kumarajiva had exhaustively studied the doctrines and philosophy of Mahayana Buddhism as systematized by Nagarjuna and other great Indian scholars. Based on these doctrines, he contemplated and realized the meaning of "the lotus blossom of the wonderful Law." Through Kumarajiva's long spiritual odyssey, he gained the ability to grasp the ultimate reality implicit in the Lotus Sutra and to express this realization through his brilliant translation. It formed the foundation of many subsequent Lotus Sutra studies.

The meaning of "Lotus Blossom of the Wonderful Law" may be gleaned in part from reading the text. But nowhere in the sutra do we find a definitive explication of the Law referred to in the title. Therein lies Nichiren's significance: he gave the Law concrete expression as Nam-myoho-renge-kyo.

Nichiren interpreted all twenty-eight chapters of the Lotus Sutra to be an elucidation of the Mystic Law, which he expressed as Nam-myoho-renge-kyo; and of the enlightenment of Shakyamuni, who had awakened to this Mystic Law. In various writings, Nichiren identified Myoho-renge-kyo equally with the ultimate reality—or absolute truth—of all phenomena and with the Buddha nature inherent in all beings.

Nichiren's assertion that the sutra's essence is inherent in its title has a long and respectable history. The earliest extant Chinese commentary on the sutra, written by one of Kumarajiva's disciples, devoted an entire section to explaining the sutra's title. More than a century later, the Great Teacher T'ien-t'ai organized all the existing Chinese Buddhist scriptures and developed a complete codification of Buddhist doctrine based on the Lotus Sutra, which, in his view, integrated all other Buddhist teachings. His ten-volume *Profound Meaning of the Lotus*

Sutra is devoted largely to explaining the title, and it concludes that the essence of the entire sutra is found in that phrase.

Nichiren underscored the all-embracing nature of the sutra's title, writing: "Included within the title, or daimoku, of Nam-myoho-renge-kyo is the entire sutra consisting of all eight volumes, twenty-eight chapters, and 69,384 characters, without the omission of a single character…. Chanting daimoku twice is the same as reading the entire sutra twice, one hundred daimoku equal one hundred readings of the sutra, and one thousand daimoku, one thousand readings of the sutra."[2]

He also wrote: "Those who chant Myoho-renge-kyo [the title of the Lotus Sutra] even without understanding its meaning realize not only the heart of the Lotus Sutra, but also the 'main cord,' or essential principle of the Buddha's lifetime teachings."[3]

And: "Our contemporaries think of the five characters of Myoho-renge-kyo only as a name, but this is not correct. It is the essence, that is, the heart of the Lotus Sutra."[4]

How, then, can we realize the truth of Myoho-renge-kyo for ourselves? Once again quoting Nichiren: "If you wish to free yourself from the sufferings of birth and death you have endured since time without beginning and to attain without fail unsurpassed enlightenment in this lifetime, you must perceive the mystic truth that is originally inherent in all living beings. This truth is Myoho-renge-kyo. Chanting Myoho-renge-kyo will therefore enable you to grasp the mystic truth innate in all life."[5]

Nichiren prefaces the five characters of Myoho-renge-kyo with *namu*, a word that derives from the Sanskrit word *namas*, meaning "devotion." (When placed in front of the **m** of a subsequent word, such as *myoho*, the **u** of *namu* is usually silent.)

In the act of chanting Nam-myoho-renge-kyo, we devote ourselves to, or harmonize our lives with, the fundamental principle of Myoho-renge-kyo. In so doing, we immediately manifest our inherent Buddha nature. It could also be said that when we chant, we tap the ninth consciousness and summon up unlimited life force.

Nam: Devoting Our Lives

Nichiren elaborated on the meaning of *nam*, writing: "*Namu* is...translated as 'dedicating one's life.' 'Dedicating one's life' means to offer one's life to the Buddha."[6] He explained that *nam* means devotion in both body and mind, in both the physical and spiritual aspects of life. An immediate question arises: To what should we devote ourselves?

In Nichiren Buddhism, there are two ways of describing the object of our devotion: the Law (the ultimate truth of Myoho-renge-kyo) and the Person (the Buddha, who has revealed the Law in his or her life). Nichiren inscribed the Gohonzon to contain and to graphically express these two aspects, leaving for posterity the realization of genius that he himself exemplified — that the Person and the Law are fundamentally one. Down the center of the Gohonzon, the characters read "Nam-myoho-renge-kyo (the Law) — Nichiren (the Person)," simply and powerfully depicting this concept of oneness. We'll explore the wondrous invention of the Gohonzon later in this chapter.

In Nichiren's teachings, *nam* indicates devotion to the Gohonzon in a bi-directional sense. We devote our lives to, or harmonize our lives with, the ultimate, unchanging reality. By harmonizing, we simultaneously bring forth infinite wisdom with which to extract boundless joy and freedom out of the uncertainties of our daily lives. We focus outwardly, but manifest from within.

Nam derives from Sanskrit, while *Myoho-renge-kyo* comes from Chinese. The amalgamation of both an Indo-European and an Eastern language in Nam-myoho-renge-kyo suggests the global appeal of Nichiren's teaching; it belongs not to a single culture but to all humankind.

Myoho: The Mystic Law

The word *myoho* means "Mystic Law." The Law (*ho*), or ultimate reality, is described as mystic (*myo*) because it is beyond all conceptions and formulations of the human mind; it is infinitely profound.

Nichiren clarified this point:

> What then does *myo* signify? It is simply the mysterious nature of our lives from moment to moment, which the mind cannot comprehend or words express. When we look into our own mind at any moment, we perceive neither color nor form to verify that it exists. Yet we still cannot say it does not exist, for many differing thoughts continually occur. The mind cannot be considered either to exist or not to exist. Life is indeed an elusive reality that transcends both the words and concepts of existence and nonexistence. It is neither existence nor nonexistence, yet exhibits the qualities of both. It is the mystic entity of the Middle Way that is the ultimate reality. *Myo* is the name given to the mystic nature of life, and *ho*, to its manifestations.[7]

Here, Nichiren interprets *myo* as the ultimate reality beyond our ability to perceive and *ho* as the world of phenomena in its ever-changing forms. The union of these two concepts, represented by the single word *myoho*, reflects the essential oneness of the ultimate reality and the world as it actually appears. According to Buddhism there is no fundamental distinction between the ultimate reality and the everyday one. If we realize this, we are awakened; otherwise we are under delusion.

Again, according to Nichiren: "When deluded, one is called an ordinary being, but when enlightened, one is called a Buddha."[8] In this context, "delusion" signifies the first nine of the Ten Worlds, from Hell to Bodhisattva, while "enlightenment" signifies the world of Buddhahood. However, the nine worlds and Buddhahood, together, are inherent in every single moment.

He further explained: "*Myo* indicates the nature of enlightenment [Buddhahood]," while *ho* indicates darkness or delusion [the first nine of the Ten Worlds]. The oneness of delusion and enlightenment is called *myoho* or the Mystic Law."[9]

This oneness of delusion and enlightenment can be illustrated thusly: Normal white blood cells destroy germs and play a crucial role in healing wounds, and so they are vital to our continued individual survival; but abnormal growth of these cells can cause potentially fatal diseases such as leukemia. White blood cells, then, have a beneficial (enlightened) aspect and a harmful (deluded) aspect — two potentials existing within each cell. Similarly, *all* phenomena have both positive and negative aspects.

As potentials, delusion (the nine worlds) and enlightenment (Buddhahood) coexist not just in our individual lives but also throughout the universe. As manifest realities, however, one of the two will be expressed in our lives, depending on whether we are awakened to the ultimate reality.

Nichiren explained that the character *myo* has three distinct meanings: to open, to be endowed and perfect, and to revive.

"To open" is to open up the darkness of delusion to reveal the Buddha nature. The lives of those who awaken to their own Buddha nature "open" to become coextensive with the universe.

"To be endowed and perfect" connotes that *myoho*, the Mystic Law, encompasses all phenomena and is inherent in all things; the Mystic Law embraces all of the Ten Worlds and all of the three thousand realms, permeating and integrating the whole of phenomenal reality. Also, "to be endowed and perfect" can be interpreted as the Mystic Law containing within itself all truths and blessings.

"To revive" is to enable all individuals to reveal their Buddhahood. For example, through the Mystic Law, everyone— even the worst evildoers—can bring forth the supreme Buddhahood from within. In a broader sense, "to revive" is another way of saying "to create value." When insentient materials such as wood and stone are transformed by human effort into a building, that is one form of revival. Another example is when we reform our lives to establish Buddhahood within and contribute to others' happiness.

Also, "to revive" signifies that when based upon the Mystic Law all other laws and teachings assume a correct perspective and reveal important aspects of the ultimate truth. Similarly, when we base our faith on the Mystic Law, all our abilities, character traits and other personal qualities come to life and are expressed in a manner that contributes to our own growth and benefits others.

Nichiren offered another interpretation of *myoho*: "Myo represents death, and *ho*, life."[10] It is difficult intellectually to conceive of our lives in the state of death and even more difficult to answer questions regarding how and where life exists after death. Even if we believe that our lives become latent in the universe, this is very difficult to understand. So death corresponds to *myo*, meaning "mystic" or "inconceivable."

Life, by contrast, expresses itself in various visible forms, according to definite patterns, manifesting one or another of the

Ten Worlds through the workings of the ten factors. Life, then, corresponds to *ho*, or law. Life and death are the two contrasting manifestations of the ultimate reality. Conversely, the ultimate reality can be seen in the everyday realities of life and death.

Renge: The Lotus Blossom

The word *renge* means "lotus blossom." The lotus is a plant of remarkable history and has been admired in many cultures and traditions. The oldest lotus fossils date back as far as the Cretaceous period, which lasted from about 144 million to about 65 million years ago. A fossil lotus unearthed in Japan's Kyoto area in 1933 is estimated to be ten thousand to twenty thousand years old, and it appears identical to the lotus plant we know today.

At Mohenjo-daro in Pakistan's Indus Valley, there are ancient ruins of what was once a major city. Archaeologists have found an artifact there known as the Great Bath, which was likely used for ritual ablution. An icon excavated there shows a woman wearing a headdress decorated with lotus flowers, indicating that the Indus Valley civilization respected the lotus.

When I met in 1985 with Dr. Karan Singh, a well-known Indian scholar, our discussion touched on the lotus flower. Because Buddhism spread throughout ancient India, I had thought that the lotus flower must be equally ubiquitous in the region. Astonishingly, Dr. Singh explained that the lotus grows only in the Himalayan region of India, an area well traveled by Shakyamuni while propounding his teaching.

Dr. Singh went on to describe the various meanings of the symbol of the lotus throughout India's long history: First, the flower signifies fertility, prosperity and longevity. Second, Brahma — the personification of the fundamental universal principle in Indian mythology — is said to have issued forth from a lotus.

Third, the lotus flower grows in mud, which shows that beauty can emerge even from things that are not beautiful. Fourth, the lotus flower remains dry as it floats on the surface of the water, which symbolizes remaining imperturbed amid the tribulations of life. Fifth, in Sanskrit writings, one praised the beauty of a woman's eyes by comparing them to lotus flowers. Sixth, the lotus flower closes at night and opens at dawn, a living metaphor for how our minds can open to a divine and sublime philosophy.

Dr. Singh's interpretations originate from the ancient Indian attitude toward the plant. The lotus flower is mentioned in the *Rig Veda*, the most ancient Indian scripture. At that time, the lotus was valued as both an ideal of beauty and a medicinal herb. Its rhizomes were considered a source of nutrition and strength and were used in various medicines. Shariputra, one of Shakyamuni's major disciples, was said to have been cured of a chronic illness with lotus rhizomes. The flower itself was used as an herbal medicine for kidney and stomach troubles, while its leaves were used to staunch bleeding.

In China, too, the lotus has flourished since antiquity along the Yellow River and in other areas. Poems in praise of the lotus appear in *Shih ching* (Book of Poetry), an anthology of some three hundred poems dating mostly from the early Chou dynasty about three thousand years ago. Because of its noble appearance, the Chinese regard the lotus as a symbol of a person's virtue, as in the eleventh-century Sung Dynasty essay "On the Love of the Lotus," by Chou Tun-i. To present someone with a lotus seed was to convey that you recognized that person's goodness and wished to keep that person's company. Also, the lotus flower has long been used in China on auspicious occasions to symbolize happiness, and its image was often emblazoned on implements used in wedding ceremonies. The flower is also a metaphor for a woman's beauty.

In Egypt, hieroglyphs representing the lotus appear in murals and papyri discovered in the Pyramids. Texts use the lotus as a symbol for the deity who confers the blessing of immortality. Stone columns with capitals decorated with lotus flowers have been excavated from the remains of ancient Egyptian temples, and the lotus embellished many other ancient Egyptian works of art and architecture. It is likely that the lotus, which bloomed profusely along the Nile, opening its flowers in the dawn, suggested itself to the ancient Egyptians as a symbol for the renewal of life.

In ancient Greece, the lotus symbol adorned temple sanctuaries. Excavations of ancient temple sites in the Olympus massif in northeastern Greece have unearthed architectural decorations that include arabesque patterns interwoven with lotus images.

Alexander the Great's expedition to India around 326 B.C.E initiated the synthesis of Buddhist culture and Hellenic civilization that eventually produced the artistic riches of the Gandhara region (now northern Pakistan and eastern Afghanistan). Gandharan artistic influence traveled eastward along the Silk Road and eventually, via China and the Korean Peninsula, reached Japan, where, during the sixth to eighth centuries, it contributed greatly to the development of Japanese art. In the diverse art works of ancient Gandhara, China and Japan, lotus petal patterns appear again and again.

In the famous Buddhist text *Questions of King Milinda*, written as a dialogue between the Indo-Greek king Menander and the Buddhist monk Nagasena that is said to have taken place some time after Alexander's expedition to India, the lotus flower appears as a metaphor for the greatness of the Buddhist teachings. The *Treatise on Great Perfection of Wisdom*, an exhaustive Mahayana work attributed to Nagarjuna, says that the reason

Buddha images picture Shakyamuni seated on lotus pedestals is that the lotus plant dignifies the seat of the Mystic Law.

The lotus flower was also extolled in Japanese literature, works such as the eighth-century *Record of Ancient Matters* and the poetry anthology known as the *Collection of Ten Thousand Leaves*. Sei Shonagon refers to the lotus blossom in her eleventh-century *Pillow Book* as being superior to other flowers. Later, in the Edo period (1600–1867), haiku became popular and often favorably referenced the lotus plant's beautiful flowers and large round leaves. To the Japanese, the lotus flower differs from other blossoms. It represents the purity and universal principle underlying all entirety existence. Mount Fuji is often likened to the eight-petalled lotus because of how its caldera looks from the air.

Lotus seeds are known to be very long-lived. Some two-thousand-year-old seeds discovered in a peat deposit in Japan were successfully germinated. Their descendants are now under cultivation in many parts of the country. It is as though lotus seeds provide a testament to the eternity of life.

In sum, human beings since ancient times have recognized the qualities of purity and eternity in the image of the lotus blossom, which likely led to its use as a symbol for the Law and for the teachings of Shakyamuni.

The Simultaneity of Cause and Effect

T'ien-t'ai explained that the word *lotus* in the Lotus Sutra's title is not only a metaphor for the Mystic Law but also the Law itself:

> [T]he name *renge* is not intended as a symbol for anything. It is the teaching expounded in the Lotus Sutra. The teaching expounded in the Lotus Sutra is pure and undefiled and

explains the subtleties of cause and effect. Therefore, it is called *renge*, or lotus. This name designates the true entity that the meditation based on the Lotus Sutra reveals, and is not a metaphor or figurative term.... But because the essence of the Lotus Sutra is difficult to understand, the metaphor of the lotus plant is introduced.... Thus the easily understood metaphor of an actual lotus plant is used to make clear the difficult-to-understand lotus that is the essence of the Lotus Sutra.[11]

Nichiren elaborated on the profound principle:

Myoho-renge-kyo is likened to the Lotus.... Of all the flowers, [the Buddha] selected the lotus blossom to symbolize the Lotus Sutra. There is a reason for this. Some plants first flower and then produce fruit, while in others fruit comes forth before flowers. Some bear only one flower but much fruit, others send forth many flowers but only one fruit, and still others produce fruit without flowering. Thus there are all manner of plants, but the lotus is the only one that bears flowers and fruit simultaneously. The benefit of all the other sutras is uncertain, because they teach that one must first make good causes and only then can one become a Buddha at some later time. With regard to the Lotus Sutra, when one's hand takes it up, that hand immediately attains Buddhahood, and when one's mouth chants it, that mouth is itself a Buddha, as, for example, the moon is reflected in the water the moment it appears from behind the eastern mountains, or as a sound and its echo arise simultaneously.[12]

He further explained:

> This passage of commentary means that the supreme prin-
> ciple [that is the Mystic Law] was originally without a name.
> When the sage was observing the principle and assigning
> names to all things, he perceived that there is this wonder-
> ful single Law [*myoho*] that simultaneously possesses both
> cause and effect [*renge*], and he named it Myoho-renge. This
> single Law that is Myoho-renge encompasses within it all
> the phenomena comprising the Ten Worlds and the three
> thousand realms, and is lacking in none of them. Anyone
> who practices this Law will obtain both the cause and the
> effect of Buddhahood simultaneously.[13]

The lotus plant produces its blossoms and its seedpods at
the same time, thereby representing "the wonderful single Law
that simultaneously possesses both cause and effect." This
principle — the simultaneity of cause and effect — means that
both the nine worlds (cause) and the world of Buddhahood
(effect) exist simultaneously in every moment of life; there is
no essential difference, therefore, between a Buddha and an
ordinary person.

Within all beings, sentient or insentient, is the Law embodying the simultaneity of cause and effect. This central theme of
Buddhism is paralleled in modern scientific theories such as the
big bang — the unimaginable explosion some twenty billion
years ago, which is generally accepted to have given birth to
our physical universe of hundreds of billions of galaxies, each
with tens or hundreds of billions of stars and planets. The universe began to expand at the very moment it came into being,
which illustrates cause and effect occurring simultaneously.

Another marvel is the fertilized human egg. No more than a

tenth of a millimeter around, it contains all the genetic information required to develop into a full-sized adult human being. At the moment of conception, the egg can be seen as simultaneously embodying both the effect and the cause of a new human being.

A plant seed likewise exemplifies the oneness of cause and effect. Seeds are generally sown in spring and bear fruit in autumn. But from a different perspective than the purely temporal one, we can say that inherent within the seed are both cause and effect. A profound contemplation of the causal law at work in life inevitably leads us to acceptance of the oneness of cause and effect.

We must bear in mind that the examples cited above deal with causality in the world of phenomena, the realm accessible to scientific investigation and confirmation. The Buddhist principle of causality, however, probes much deeper, penetrating the innermost nooks and crannies of life. It deals with a realm transcending space and time. From that perspective, then, it is meaningless to talk of cause preceding effect: both exist simultaneously.

People sometimes equate causality—either the scientific or the karmic concept—with determinism, the belief that there is no free will. This is likely from their conception that a given cause must inevitably produce a given effect, which one can do little about. The deterministic view, however, fails to account for our potential to alter the meanings of our past deeds through the causes or actions we initiate from now on.

Buddhism teaches that there is an indispensable element necessary for bringing to the surface the causality dormant in the depths of our being. This element is an external cause that, when it unites with a latent cause, produces a manifest effect. Without the appropriate external cause, the latent cause and the latent effect coexisting with it remain forever dormant.

Moreover, depending on the nature of the external cause—for example, our interaction with the environment—latent effects become manifest in a variety of forms. As we bring forth the supreme condition of Buddhahood from within ourselves, the entire network of causes and effects comprising our personal destiny or life-condition is dramatically transformed, becoming Buddhahood-based rather than delusion-based and working to advance our development as human beings.

Mortal Desires and the Purity of the Lotus

Another attribute of the lotus that lends itself to Buddhist symbolism is that it grows and blooms in muddy water, yet its blossoms are pure and beautiful. Similarly, the pure Buddha nature emerges from within the lives of ordinary persons, despite their delusions and desires. "Emerging from the Earth," the fifteenth chapter of the Lotus Sutra, describes people who embrace the Mystic Law as "unsoiled by worldly things / like the lotus flower in the water."[14] This concept involves one of the cardinal concerns of Buddhism.

Human existence is often seen as a seething whirlpool of desires, drives and impulses that give rise to vices and suffering. Those dominated solely by their desires and impulses can enjoy neither true self-identity nor freedom. Instead, they will always be at the mercy of changing circumstances. For this reason, some religious teachings claim that the eradication of desire is the sole path to salvation.

Desire is an inherent function of life. Ultimately, we cannot extinguish desire without extinguishing life itself. But the innate function of desire within our individual lives can be thought of as neutral; it has the potential either to harm or to benefit human existence. Rather than suppress our desires, the real question is how to control and direct them so that they enhance human virtues.

This is where Buddhism comes in. According to Buddhist teachings, once we activate the supreme state of Buddhahood inherent in each of us, the workings of our desires are redirected toward furthering our individual growth and enlightenment. If, by contrast, we give our desires free rein without first orienting them in a higher state of life, they will only operate destructively, bringing us anguish and perhaps even threatening our continued existence.

The significance of Buddhism lies both in the discovery of the Buddha nature in all beings and in the establishment of a practical method for bringing it out, so that human beings can derive maximum meaning from their lives. Both these features are especially relevant to modern civilization, which has long been trapped in a sort of spiritual quicksand. We can escape the quicksand by calling forth the supreme human potential available to each of us. Desires, if properly channeled, can fuel our spiritual development. If they are improperly channeled, they become a liability.

Kyo: The Buddha's Teaching

The word *kyo* is the Japanese translation of "sutra," a teaching of Shakyamuni. Because the Buddha taught through preaching — that is, he used his own voice — the word *kyo* has sometimes been interpreted as "sound." T'ien-t'ai wrote: "The voice does the Buddha's work and is therefore termed *kyo*."[15] Nichiren also taught: "*Kyo* means the words and speech, sounds and voices of all living beings."[16]

The Chinese character for *kyo* originally meant the warp of a length of cloth. Possibly because this creates the image of

continuity, *kyo* also came to mean a teaching to be preserved
and handed down for posterity. The character was used in China
to mean "books" or "classics," such as those of Confucianism or
Taoism; and when the Buddhist scriptures were introduced from
India, the character was used to mean "sutra." It is in this sense
that Nichiren interprets the word when he says, "That which is
eternal, spanning [past, present and future], is called *kyo*."

With his magnificent voice, Shakyamuni profoundly inspired
people and revived their spirits. His was a voice of truth that
expressed the Law to which he had awakened in the depths of
his being. The voice is the vibration of the whole living entity;
it reveals a person's being and character. Nam-myoho-renge-kyo
is the fundamental rhythm of the universe, the greatest voice of
all. Again, according to Nichiren: "When once we chant
Myoho-renge-kyo, with just that single sound we summon forth
and manifest the Buddha nature of all Buddhas...and all other
living beings. This blessing is immeasurable and boundless."[17]

Elsewhere, he wrote: "Nichiren alone, without sparing his
voice, now chants Nam-myoho-renge-kyo."[18] "Without sparing
his voice," refers not to loudness but rather to the great voice of
compassion that seeks to bring all beings to enlightenment.

A Buddha's enlightenment, expressed through the voice, is
kyo, and the truth to which a Buddha has been enlightened is
eternal, spanning past, present and future. When we awaken to
this truth we realize the eternal aspect of our individual lives, an
aspect that transcends the changes of the physical world and
the cycle of birth and death.

The Gohonzon: Object of Devotion

The Law of Nam-myoho-renge-kyo, which encompasses all
phenomena in the universe and perfectly expresses their

unchanging reality, is embodied in the Gohonzon. Down the center, in Chinese characters, it reads "Nam-myoho-renge-kyo —Nichiren." On either side of that center inscription, in Chinese and medieval Sanskrit, there are characters for the names of beings representing each of the Ten Worlds. All these names express the principles that the Ten Worlds exist within the eternal Buddha's life and that living beings of the Ten Worlds can attain Buddhahood.·

One reason the object of devotion consists of writing is that it would be impossible to depict the mutual possession of the Ten Worlds in a graphic image even though each world could be depicted separately.

The universe includes the powers of both good and evil. In the Gohonzon, all of the Ten Worlds are represented, from the Buddha realm to the state of Hell. The light of Nam-myoho-renge-kyo illuminates equally the powers and capacities of good and evil; both good and evil display the "exalted form that inherently exists in them," another way of saying existence just as it is.

The exalted form of fundamental existence is given appearance in this world as the Gohonzon. Therefore, when we chant before the Gohonzon, the good and evil (or deluded) capacities of our lives begin to function as the exalted form of fundamental existence. Lives filled with the pain of Hell, lives warped by the state of Anger—such lives, too, begin to move toward creating personal happiness and value. Lives being pulled toward misfortune and unhappiness are redirected toward good when the Mystic Law is made their base. It is as if sufferings are made the fuel for a fire of joy, wisdom and compassion. The Mystic Law and faith ignite the flame.

It goes without saying that the worlds of good—such states as Buddhahood, Bodhisattva and Heaven—only increase their brightness and their efficacy through the power of chanting Nam-myoho-renge-kyo. Good and evil, all the three thousand realms and factors of existence merge and lead us to happiness, to a life of eternity, joy, true self and purity.

Through faith in the Gohonzon and the chanting of Nam-myoho-renge-kyo, we can bring forth the Buddhahood that is the ultimate reality of each of our lives. Thus, the Mystic Law is both the object of devotion and, more generally, the truth inherent within us. Nichiren explained this in a letter to a follower named Abutsu-bo:

> At present the entire body of the Honorable Abutsu is composed of the five elements of earth, water, fire, wind, and space. These five elements are also the five characters of the daimoku. Abutsu-bo is therefore the treasure tower itself, and the treasure tower is Abutsu-bo himself. No other knowledge is purposeful. It is the treasure tower adorned with the seven kinds of treasures — hearing the correct teaching, believing it, keeping the precepts, engaging in meditation, practicing assiduously, renouncing one's attachments, and reflecting on oneself.[19]

As explained in chapter one, the treasure tower is the great metaphor of the Lotus Sutra that represents the infinite potential for happiness within each individual's life, coextensive with the infinite cosmos. The treasure tower is synonymous with the Mystic Law, or the Gohonzon, or the Buddha nature inherent within each of us.

In this passage, Nichiren related "the entire body of [Abutsu-bo]" to Myoho-renge-kyo, or the Mystic Law. The Mystic Law exists nowhere outside the world of phenomena, the world of the five universal elements; the Mystic Law is inseparable from our bodies. Indeed, our bodies — as the manifestations of our lives — are also entities of the Mystic Law. The body and the mind are inseparable and essentially indistinguishable; they are a single entity. When Buddhism makes mention of the human body, it is not referring to the physical body as distinct from the mind, it is the whole entity that incorporates both mind and body.

It is difficult to believe that our bodies themselves are the Mystic Law, and so too often we waste our efforts trying to find it elsewhere. Yet through applying ourselves to Buddhist practice, we can each achieve the same level of awareness as Nichiren, who explained that the treasure tower represents the Gohonzon as well as the lives of those who embrace it and thereby reveal their innate Buddha nature.

The Gohonzon embodies a truth, the unchanging reality of ever-changing phenomena, and the existence of the profoundest condition of life that is latent within us. For this reason, Nichiren also wrote: "Never seek this Gohonzon outside yourself. The Gohonzon exists only within the mortal flesh of us ordinary people who embrace the Lotus Sutra and chant Nam-myoho-renge-kyo."[20]

Looking Ahead

Buddhism aims to free us from the sufferings of birth and death by providing us with the means to awaken to the unchanging truth — our own Buddha nature. Earlier systems of Buddhism taught that people could be brought to Buddhahood through tremendous effort in doctrinal studies and meditative disciplines, thereby restricting Buddhahood to a monastic elite. By contrast, the teachings of Nichiren demonstrate that all of us, whatever our ability or circumstances, have access to the ultimate truth.

Practicing the principles of Nichiren Buddhism, crystallized in the chanting of Nam-myoho-renge-kyo, we undergo the process of human revolution, whereby we regain control over what we might heretofore have been resigned to as our fate.

As we have seen, by grappling with the realities of daily life based on Nichiren Buddhist teachings, we can establish a state of absolute and indestructible happiness independent of our present circumstances. Brimming with vitality and confidence, we can meet and surmount all challenges to come—especially the sufferings related to sickness, aging and death. We can awaken, and awaken to, our own boundless potential and fulfill our dreams.

Hand in hand with (and inseparable from) our personal awakening, the aim of Buddhist practice is to establish a truly peaceful society based on the empowerment of all individuals, a true state of equality and justice grounded in respect for the Buddha nature inherent in everyone.

Notes

INTRODUCTION

1. Gosho Translation Committee, ed., *The Writings of Nichiren Daishonin* (Tokyo: Soka Gakkai, 1999), p. 358.

2. Ibid., p. 358.

3. Nichiko Hori, ed., *Nichiren Daishonin Gosho Zenshu* (Tokyo: Soka Gakkai, 1952), p. 740.

CHAPTER ONE: BIRTH

1. J.W. Goethe, *Faust A Tragedy*, trans. Bayard Taylor (New York: The Modern Library, 1967), pp. 17–18.

2. J. Takakusu, ed., *Nanden Daizokyo* (Tokyo: Taisho Shinshu Daizokyo Publishing Society, 1935), vol. 13, p. 1ff.

3. Ibid., vol. 23, p. 42.

4. J. Takakusu, ed., *Taisho Issaikyo* (Tokyo: Taisho Issaikyo Publishing Society, 1925), vol. 1, 645c, p. 15b.

5. Nichiko Hori, ed., *Nichiren Daishonin Gosho Zenshu* (Tokyo: Soka Gakkai, 1952), p. 1404.

6. Ibid., p. 740.

7. Ibid.

8. Ibid., p. 797.

9. From: Contemplation on the Mind-Ground Sutra (Jpn Shinjikan-gyo).

10. Gosho Translation Committee, ed., *The Writings of Nichiren Daishonin* (Tokyo: Soka Gakkai, 1999), p. 644.

11. Translated from Japanese: From Goethe's diary (1812). Ludwig von Bertalanffy, *Seimei* (Life), trans. Kei Nagano and Mamoru Iijima (Tokyo: Miscuzu shobo, 1974), p. 59.

12. Guy Murchie, *The Seven Mysteries of Life* (Boston: Houghton-Mifflin Company, 1978), p. 53.

Chapter Two: Aging

1. The quote reads: "Life is the most precious of all treasures. Even one extra day of life is worth more than ten million ryo of gold." Gosho Translation Committee, ed., *The Writings of Nichiren Daishonin* (Tokyo: Soka Gakkai, 1999), p. 955.

2. Ibid., p. 851.

3. *The New York Times*, Feb. 21, 1984.

4. Ibid.

5. Ibid.

6. Ibid.

7. Morton Puner, *To the Good Long Life: What We Know About Growing Old* (New York: Universe Books, 1975).

8. *The Writings of Nichiren Daishonin*, p. 413.

9. Nichiko Hori, ed., *Nichiren Daishonin Gosho Zenshu* (Tokyo: Soka Gakkai, 1952), p. 790.

10. Burton Watson, trans., *The Lotus Sutra* (New York: Columbia University Press, 1993), p. 228.

11. *Gosho Zenshu*, p. 1458.

Chapter Three: Illness and the Medicine of Buddhism

1. Gosho Translation Committee, ed., *The Writings of Nichiren Daishonin* (Tokyo: Soka Gakkai, 1999), p. 851.

2. Second president of the Soka Gakkai; see Introduction.

3. *The Writings of Nichiren Daishonin*, p. 952.

4. Ibid., p. 447.

5. Ibid., p. 937.

6. Ibid., p. 218.

7. Ibid., p. 149.

8. Ibid., p. 146.

9. Ibid., p. 145.

CHAPTER FOUR: DEATH

1. Nichiko Hori, ed., *Nichiren Daishonin Gosho Zenshu* (Tokyo: Soka Gakkai, 1952), p. 1404.

2. Burton Watson, trans., *The Lotus Sutra* (New York: Columbia University Press, 1993), p. 230.

3. *Gosho Zenshu*, p. 788.

4. *Toda Josei Zenshu* (The Collected Works of Josei Toda) (Tokyo: Seikyo Shimbunsha, 1983), vol. 3, pp. 5–12.

5. Ibid.

6. Raymond A. Moody, Jr., *Life After Life* (Atlanta: Macmillan Publishing, 1975), pp. 29–30.

7. *Gosho Zenshu*, p. 984.

8. Gosho Translation Committee, ed., *The Writings of Nichiren Daishonin* (Tokyo: Soka Gakkai, 1999), p. 218.

9. *Gosho Zenshu*, pp. 569–70.

10. Ibid., pp. 1508–09.

11. *The Writings of Nichiren Daishonin*, p. 216.

12. Ibid., pp. 395–96.

13. Ibid., pp. 760–61.

14. *Gosho Zenshu*, p. 574.

15. *The Lotus Sutra*, pp. 69–70.

16. *Taisho Shinshu Daizokyo* (Tokyo: Taisho Shinshu Daizokyo Publishing Society, 1935), vol. 12, p. 497.

17. *The Lotus Sutra*, p. 226.

18. *Gosho Zenshu*, p. 754.

19. J.P. Eckermann, *Conversations with Goethe*, trans. Gisela C. O'Brien (New York: Frederick Ungar Publishing Co., 1964), p. 33.

CHAPTER FIVE: LIFE'S UNLIMITED POTENTIAL

1. Burton Watson, trans., *The Lotus Sutra* (New York: Columbia University Press, 1993), p. 229.

2. Ibid., p. 226.

3. Gosho Translation Committee, ed., *The Writings of Nichiren Daishonin* (Tokyo: Soka Gakkai, 1999), p. 358.

4. *Kokuyaku Issaikyo Indo Senutsubu Ronshubu*, vol., 1, ed. Shinyu Iwano (Tokyo: Daito Shuppansha, 1977), p. 114.

5. Fyodor Dostoevsky, *The Brothers Karamazov* (New York: Random House, 1943, 1945), p. 283.

6. Nichiko Hori, ed., *Nichiren Daishonin Gosho Zenshu* (Tokyo: Soka Gakkai, 1952), p. 761.

7. *The Writings of Nichiren Daishonin*, p. 358.

8. Ibid., p. 224.

9. Ibid., p. 358.

10. Ibid., p. 486.

11. Ibid., p. 681.

12. *The Lotus Sutra*, p. 24.

13. *The Writings of Nichiren Daishonin*, p. 354.

14. Ibid., p. 184.

15. Ibid., p. 356.

16. Norman Cousins, *Human Options* (New York: W.W. Norton, Inc., 1981).

17. *The Writings of Nichiren Daishonin*, p. 644.

18. Ibid., p. 4.

19. René Dubos, *Man Adapting* (New Haven: Yale University Press, 1969), p. 342.

20. *The Writings of Nichiren Daishonin*, p. 629.

21. *Gosho Zenshu*, p. 567.

22. From: T'ien-t'ai, *Words and Phrases of the Lotus Sutra*.

Chapter Six: The Nine Consciousnesses

1. Burton Watson, trans., *The Lotus Sutra* (New York: Columbia University Press, 1993), p. 251.

2. Helen Keller, *Midstream: My Later Life* (New York: Doubleday, Doran & Company, Inc., 1929), p. 49.

3. Helen Keller, *The Story of My Life* (New York: Doubleday & Company, Inc., 1954), p. 254.

4. *Toda Josei Zenshu* (The Collected Works of Josei Toda) (Tokyo: Seikyo Shimbunsha, 1985), vol. 5, p. 412.

5. Gosho Translation Committee, ed., *The Writings of Nichiren Daishonin* (Tokyo: Soka Gakkai, 1999), p. 832.

6. Ibid., p. 458.

7. *Toda Josei Zenshu* (The Collected Works of Josei Toda) (Tokyo: Seikyo Shimbunsha, 1984), vol. 4, p. 259.

Chapter Seven: Nam-myoho-renge-kyo

1. Gosho Translation Committee, ed., *The Writings of Nichiren Daishonin* (Tokyo: Soka Gakkai, 1999), p. 317.

2. Ibid., pp. 922–23.

3. Ibid., p. 860.

4. Ibid., p. 861.

5. Ibid., p. 3.

6. Ibid., p. 1125.

7. Ibid., p. 4.

8. Ibid.

9. Nichiko Hori, ed., *Nichiren Daishonin Gosho Zenshu* (Tokyo: Soka Gakkai, 1952), p. 708.

10. *The Writings of Nichiren Daishonin*, p. 216.

11. Ibid., p. 421.

12. Ibid., p. 1099.

13. Ibid., p. 421.

14. Burton Watson, trans., *The Lotus Sutra* (New York: Columbia University Press, 1993), p. 222.

15. From: T'ien-t'ai, *Profound Meaning of the Lotus Sutra*.

16. *Gosho Zenshu*, p. 708.

17. *The Writings of Nichiren Daishonin*, p. 887.

18. Ibid., p. 736.

19. Ibid., p. 299.

20. Ibid., p. 832.

Glossary

bodhisattva (Skt; Jpn *bosatsu*) One who aspires to enlightenment, or Buddhahood. *Bodhi* means enlightenment, and *sattva*, a living being. A person who aspires to enlightenment and carries out altruistic practice. The predominant characteristic of a bodhisattva is therefore compassion. Bodhisattvas make four universal vows: (1) to save innumerable living beings, (2) to eradicate countless earthly desires, (3) to master immeasurable Buddhist teachings, and (4) to attain the supreme enlightenment.

Buddhahood (Jpn *bukkai*) The state that a Buddha has attained. The ultimate goal of Buddhist practice and the highest of the Ten Worlds. The word *enlightenment* is often used synonymously with Buddhahood. Buddhahood is regarded as a state of perfect freedom, in which one is awakened to the eternal and ultimate truth that is the reality of all things. This supreme state of life is characterized by boundless wisdom and infinite compassion. The Lotus Sutra reveals that Buddhahood is a potential in the lives of all beings.

cause and effect (1) Buddhism expounds the law of cause and effect that operates in life, ranging over past, present and future existences. This causality underlies the doctrine of karma. From this viewpoint, causes formed in the past are manifested as effects in the present. Causes formed in the present will be manifested as effects in the future. (2) From the viewpoint of Buddhist practice, cause represents the bodhisattva practice for attaining Buddhahood, and effect represents the benefit of Buddhahood. (3) From the viewpoint that, among the Ten Worlds, cause represents the nine worlds and effect represents Buddhahood, Nichiren refers to two kinds of teachings: those that view things from the standpoint of "cause to effect" and those that approach things from the standpoint of "effect to cause." The former indicates Shakyamuni's teaching, by which ordinary persons carry out

Buddhist practice (cause) aiming at the goal of Buddhahood (effect). In contrast, the latter indicates Nichiren's teaching, in which ordinary persons manifest their innate Buddhahood (effect) through faith and practice, and then, based on Buddhahood, go out among the people of the nine worlds (cause) to lead them to Buddhahood.

daimoku (Jpn) (1) The title of a sutra, in particular the title of the Lotus Sutra of the Wonderful Law (Chin *Miao-fa-lien-hua-ching*; Jpn *Myoho-renge-kyo*). The title of a sutra represents the essence of the sutra. (2) The invocation of Nam-myoho-renge-kyo in Nichiren's teachings. One of his Three Great Secret Laws.

dependent origination (Skt *pratitya-samutpada*; Pali *paticcha- samuppada*; Jpn *engi* or *innen*) Also, dependent causation or conditioned co-arising. A Buddhist doctrine expressing the interdependence of all things. It teaches that no being or phenomenon exists on its own, but exists or occurs because of its relationship with other beings or phenomena. Everything in the world comes into existence in response to causes and conditions. In other words, nothing can exist independent of other things or arise in isolation.

Dharma (Skt; Pali *dhamma*; Jpn *ho*) A term fundamental to Buddhism that derives from a verbal root *dhri*, which means to preserve, maintain, keep, or uphold. *Dharma* has a wide variety of meanings, such as law, truth, doctrine, the Buddha's teaching, decree, observance, conduct, duty, virtue, morality, religion, justice, nature, quality, character, characteristic, essence, elements of existence, and phenomena. Some of the more common usages are: (1) (Often capitalized) The Law, or ultimate truth. For example, Kumarajiva translated *saddharma*, the Sanskrit word that literally means correct Law, as Wonderful Law or Mystic Law, indicating the unfathomable truth or Law that governs all phenomena. (2) The teaching of the Buddha that reveals the Law. The *Dharma* of *abhidharma* means the Buddha's doctrine, or the sutras. (3) (Often plural) Manifestations of the Law, i.e., phenomena, things, facts, or existences. The word "phenomena" in "the true aspect of all phenomena" is the translation of *dharmas*. (4) The elements of existence, which, according to the Hinayana schools, are the most basic constituents of the individual and his or her reality. (5) Norms of conduct leading to the accumulation of good karma.

earthly desires (Skt *klesha*; Pali *kilesa*; Jpn *bonno*) Also, illusions, defilements, impurities, earthly passions, or simply desires. A generic term for all the workings of life, including desires and illusions in the general sense, that cause one psychological and physical suffering and impede the quest for enlightenment.

expedient means (Skt *upaya*; Jpn *hoben*) The methods adopted to instruct people and lead them to enlightenment. The concept of expedient means is highly regarded in Mahayana Buddhism, especially in the Lotus Sutra, as represented by its second chapter entitled "Expedient Means." This is because expedient means are skillfully devised and employed by Buddhas and bodhisattvas to lead the people to salvation.

four noble truths A fundamental doctrine of Buddhism clarifying the cause of suffering and the way of emancipation. The four noble truths are the truth of suffering, the truth of the origin of suffering, the truth of the cessation of suffering, and the truth of the path to the cessation of suffering.

four sufferings (Jpn *shi-ku*) The four universal sufferings: birth, aging, sickness and death. Various sutras describe Shakyamuni's quest for enlightenment as being motivated by a desire to find a solution to these four sufferings.

Gohonzon (Jpn) The object of devotion. The word *go* is an honorific pre- fix, and *honzon* means object of fundamental respect or devotion. In Nichiren's teaching, the object of devotion has two aspects: the object of devotion in terms of the Law and the object of devotion in terms of the Person. It takes the form of a mandala inscribed on paper or on wood with characters representing the Mystic Law as well as the Ten Worlds. Nichiren Buddhism holds that all people possess the Buddha nature and can attain Buddhahood through faith in the Gohonzon.

human revolution A concept coined by the Soka Gakkai's second pres- ident, Josei Toda, to indicate the self-reformation of an individual— the strengthening of life force and the establishment of Buddhahood—that is the goal of Buddhist practice.

karma Potential energies residing in the inner realm of life, which man- ifest themselves as various results in the future. In Buddhism, karma is interpreted as meaning mental, verbal and physical action; that is, thoughts, words and deeds.

Kumarajiva (344–413 c.e.) Translator of the Lotus Sutra into Chinese.

Lotus Sutra The highest teaching of Shakyamuni Buddha, it reveals that all people can attain enlightenment and declares that his former teachings should be regarded as preparatory.

Many Treasures Also referred to as Taho Buddha. A Buddha who appears, seated within the treasure tower, at the Ceremony in the Air to bear witness to the truth of Shakyamuni's teachings in the Lotus Sutra.

Miao-lo The sixth patriarch in the lineage of the T'ien-t'ai school in China, counting from the Great Teacher T'ien-t'ai. Miao-lo reasserted the supremacy of the Lotus Sutra and wrote commentaries on T'ien-t'ai's three major works, thus bringing about a revival of interest in T'ien-t'ai Buddhism. He is revered as the restorer of the school.

mutual possession of the Ten Worlds The principle that each of the Ten Worlds contains all the other nine as potential within itself. This is taken to mean that an individual's state of life can be changed, and that all beings of the nine worlds possess the potential for Buddhahood. *See also* Ten Worlds.

Mystic Law The ultimate law of life and the universe. The law of Nam-myoho-renge-kyo. *See also* Nam-myoho-renge-kyo.

Nam-myoho-renge-kyo The ultimate law of the true aspect of life permeating all phenomena in the universe. The invocation established by Nichiren on April 28, 1253. Nichiren teaches that this phrase encompasses all laws and teachings within itself, and that the benefit of chanting Nam-myoho-renge-kyo includes the benefit of conducting all virtuous practices. *Nam* means "devotion to"; *myoho* means "Mystic Law"; *renge* refers to the lotus flower, which simultaneously blooms and seeds, indicating the simultaneity of cause and effect; *kyo* means sutra, the teaching of a Buddha.

Nichiren The thirteenth-century Japanese Buddhist teacher and reformer who taught that all people have the potential for enlightenment. He defined the universal Law as Nam-myoho-renge-kyo and established the Gohonzon as the object of devotion for all people to attain Buddhahood.

nine consciousnesses Nine kinds of discernment. "Consciousness" is the translation of the Sanskrit *vijnana*, which means discernment. The nine consciousnesses are (1) sight-consciousness, (2) hearing-consciousness, (3) smell-consciousness, (4) taste-consciousness, (5) touch-consciousness, (6) mind-consciousness, (7) *mano*-consciousness, (8) *alaya*-consciousness, and (9) *amala*-consciousness. The first five correspond to the five senses of sight, hearing, smell, taste and touch. The sixth consciousness integrates the perceptions of the five senses into coherent images and makes judgments. The seventh consciousness corresponds to the inner spiritual world. The eighth consciousness exists in what modern psychology calls the unconscious, where all experiences of present and previous lifetimes—collectively called karma—are stored. The ninth consciousness is defined as the basis of all spiritual functions and is identified with the true entity of life.

nirvana   Enlightenment, the ultimate goal of Buddhist practice.

non-substantiality   (Jpn) A fundamental Buddhist concept, variously translated as emptiness, void, latency, relativity, etc. The concept that entities have no fixed or independent nature.

oneness of life and environment   The principle stating that the self and its environment are two integral phases of the same entity.

oneness of body and mind (Jpn shikishin-funi)   Also, non-duality of body and mind. The principle that the two seemingly distinct phenomena of body, or the physical aspect of life, and mind, or its spiritual aspect, are essentially non-dual, being two integral phases of a single reality.

Shakyamuni   Also, Siddhartha Gautama. Born in India (present-day southern Nepal) about three thousand years ago, he is the first recorded Buddha and founder of Buddhism. For fifty years, he expounded various sutras (teachings), culminating in the Lotus Sutra.

Soka Gakkai International   A worldwide Buddhist association that promotes peace and individual happiness based on the teachings of the Nichiren school of Buddhism, with more than twelve million members in 163 countries. Its headquarters is in Tokyo, Japan.

ten factors   Ten factors common to all life in any of the Ten Worlds. They are: (1) Appearance: attributes of things discernible from the outside. (2) Nature: the inherent disposition or quality of a thing or being that cannot be discerned from the outside. (3) Entity: the essence of life that permeates and integrates appearance and nature. (4) Power: life's potential energy. (5) Influence: the action or movement produced when life's inherent power is activated. (6) Internal cause: the cause latent in life that produces an effect of the same quality as itself, i.e., good, evil or neutral. (7) Relation: the relationship of indirect causes to the internal cause. (8) Latent effect: the effect produced in life when an internal cause is activated through its relationship with various conditions. (9) Manifest effect: the tangible, perceivable result that emerges in time as an expression of a latent effect and therefore of an internal cause, again through its relationship with various conditions. (10) Consistency from beginning to end: the unifying factor among the ten factors. It indicates that all of the other nine factors are consistently and harmoniously interrelated. All nine factors thus express the same condition of existence at any given moment.

Ten Worlds   Ten life-conditions that a single entity of life manifests. Originally the Ten Worlds were viewed as distinct physical places, each with its own particular inhabitants. In light of the Lotus Sutra, they are interpreted as potential conditions of life inherent in each individual. The ten are: (1) Hell, (2) Hunger, (3) Animality, (4) Anger, (5) Humanity or Tranquillity, (6) Rapture, (7) Learning, (8) Realization, (9) Bodhisattva and (10) Buddhahood.

treasure tower   A tower or stupa adorned with treasures or jewels. Any of a variety of jeweled stupas depicted in Buddhist scriptures. Nichiren viewed the treasure tower as an allegory for human life in its enlightened state achieved through the chanting of Nam-myoho-renge-kyo. He also refers to the Gohonzon, the object of devotion in his teaching, as "the treasure tower."

three thousand realms in a single moment of life   (*ichinen sanzen*) Also, the principle of a single moment of life comprising three thousand realms. "A single moment of life" is also translated as one mind, one thought, or one thought-moment. A philosophical system established by T'ien-t'ai (538–597) in his *Great Concentration and Insight* on the basis of the phrase "the true aspect of all phenomena" from the "Expedient Means" chapter of the Lotus Sutra. The number three thousand here comes from the following calculation: 10 (Ten Worlds) x 10 (Ten Worlds) x 10 (ten factors) x 3 (three realms of existence). Life at any moment manifests one of the Ten Worlds. Each of these worlds possesses the potential for all ten within itself, and this "mutual possession" of the Ten Worlds is represented as a hundred possible worlds. Each of these hundred worlds possesses the ten factors, making one thousand factors or potentials, and these operate within each of the three realms of existence, thus making three thousand realms.

three realms of existence   The realm of the five components, the realm of living beings, and the realm of the environment. The concept of three realms of existence views life from three different standpoints and explains the existence of individual lives in the real world. These realms themselves are not to be viewed separately but as aspects of an integrated whole, which simultaneously manifests any of the Ten Worlds.

Index

Also from Middleway Press

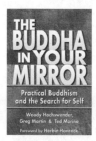

The Buddha in Your Mirror: Practical Buddhism and the Search for Self, by Woody Hochswender, Greg Martin and Ted Morino (ISBN0-9674697-8-3; $14.00)

Also available in Spanish: *El Buda en tu Espejo* (ISBN 0-9674697-7-5; $14.00)

"Like the Buddha, this book offers practical guide-lines to overcome difficulties in everyday life and to be helpful to others. Readers will find these pages are like a helpful and supportive friend. I enthusiastically recommend it."

—DR. DAVID CHAPPELL, EDITOR OF
BUDDHIST PEACEWORK: CREATING CULTURES OF PEACE

For the Sake of Peace: Seven Paths to Global Harmony, A Buddhist Perspective, by Daisaku Ikeda

Winner of the NAPRA Nautilus Award 2002 for Social Change (ISBN 0-9674697-9-1; $14.00)

"At a time when we squander enormous amounts of human and environmental resources on the study of and preparation for making war, *For the Sake of Peace* stands as a primary text in the study and practice of making peace."   —NAPRA, NAUTILUS AWARD CITATION

On Being Human: Where Ethics, Medicine and Spirituality Converge by Daisaku Ikeda, René Simard and Guy Bourgeault (ISBN 0-9723267-1-5; $15.95)

"ON BEING HUMAN is an elegant and timely dialogue. Accessible yet profound, it illustrates the convergence of medical science, bioethics and Buddhist philosophy. Informative and hopeful, it offers wise perspectives on life and death, revealing their deeper meaning and higher purpose. Its three sagacious voices speak as one, to all."

— LOU MARINOFF, AUTHOR OF
Plato Not Prozac and *The Big Questions*

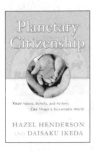

Planetary Citizenship: Your Values, Beliefs and Actions Can Shape a Sustainable World by Hazel Henderson and Daisaku Ikeda (ISBN 0-9723267-2-3; $23.95)

"*Planetary Citizenship* is a delightful introduction to some of the most important ideas and facts concerning stewardship of the planet. I cannot think of any book that deals with more important issues."

— MIHALY CSIKSZENTMIHALYI, AUTHOR OF
Flow: The Psychology of Optimal Experience

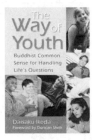

The Way of Youth: Buddhist Common Sense for Handling Life's Questions, by Daisaku Ikeda (ISBN 0-9674697-0-8; $14.95)

Also available in Spanish: *A la Manera de los Jovenés* (ISBN 0-9674697-3-2; $14.95)

"[This book] shows the reader how to flourish as a young person in the world today; how to build confidence and character in modern society; learn to live with respect for oneself and others; how to contribute to a positive, free and peaceful society; and find true personal happiness."

—MIDWEST BOOK REVIEW

ASK FOR MIDDLEWAY PRESS BOOKS AT YOUR FAVORITE NEIGHBORHOOD OR ON-LINE BOOKSELLER.
OR VISIT WWW.MIDDLEWAYPRESS.COM.

green
press
INITIATIVE

Printed on recycled paper

MIDDLEWAY PRESS IS COMMITTED to preserving ancient forest and natural resources. We are a member of Green Press Initiative—a nonprofit program dedicated to supporting book publishers in maximizing their use of fiber which is not sourced from ancient or endangered forests. We have elected to print this title on New Leaf EcoBook 100, made with 100% recycled fiber, processed chlorine free. For more information about Green Press Initiative and the use of recycled paper in book publishing, visit www.greenpressinitiative.org.

 NEW LEAF PAPER
ENVIRONMENTAL BENEFITS STATEMENT

Unlocking the Mysteries of Birth & Death is printed on New Leaf EcoBook 100, made with 100% post-consumer waste, processed chlorine free. By using this environmentally friendly paper, the following resources were saved:

trees	water	energy	solid waste	greenhouse gases
55 fully grown	23,622 gallons	40 million BTUs	5,191 pounds	4,538 pounds

Calculated based on research done by Environmental Defense and other members of the Paper Task Force.

© New Leaf Paper   Visit us in cyberspace at www.newleafpaper.com or call 1-888-989-5323